to

....

from

....

the Romantic Vegetarian

Enticing menus in seductive settings
for love and romance through the year.

the Romantic Vegetarian

Colin Spencer

THORSONS PUBLISHING GROUP

Wellingborough, Northamptonshire

First published 1988

British Library Cataloguing in Publication Data

Spencer, Colin
The romantic vegetarian.
1. Vegetarian cookery
I. Title
641.5'636   TX837

ISBN 0-7225-1327-5

Published by Thorsons Publishers Limited,
Wellingborough, Northamptonshire, NN8 2RQ, England

Printed and bound in Portugal by Printer Portuguesa Lda.

1 3 5 7 9 10 8 6 4 2

Contents

'To be born into this earth is to be born into uncongenial surroundings, hence to be born into a romance.'

G. K. Chesterton

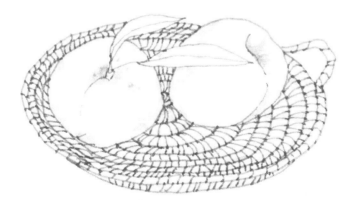

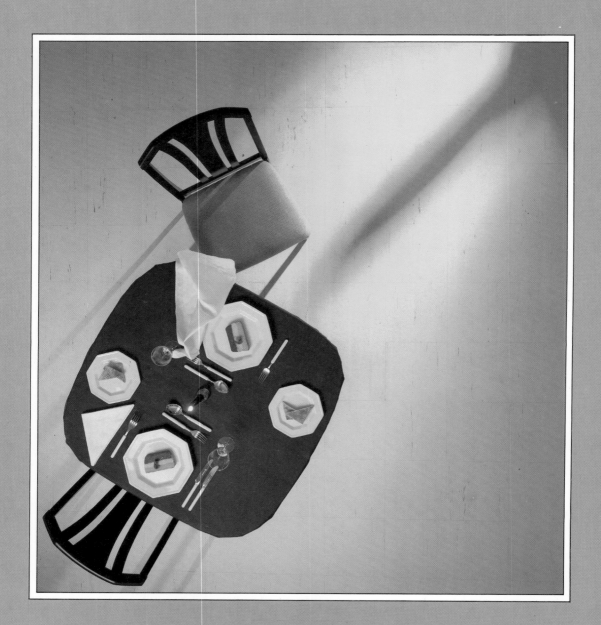

Bon appetit!

Preface

What is romance? The accepted notion is a highly sentimentalized, almost slavish devotion equal between two people, which contains an element of magic because it is a heightened awareness, a kind of modified hysteria. That this is shared equally seems somewhat miraculous and, because it is shared, it is also rare. Yet the previous quotation from Chesterton places the idea of romance in a far more comprehensive, almost mythological sense and this is the tradition which lies behind the word. To narrow it down to dinners *à deux* between lovers without being aware of the larger meanings of the word would be to demean the experience.

So this book suggests an event for each month and attempts to pick the music, setting, the scent, the flowers and colours, as well as the food to celebrate two lovers dining together.

It seems to me right that the food they eat is free from fish, fowl or meat — that no blood has been spilt for their feast; that, as lovers, they are in harmony with life and the world, that they are on the side of Creation.

Introduction

Though we are conscious that the relationship between eating and sexual desire is an inter-twined one, we do not examine it too closely for fear, I suspect, that one or the other may well vanish. The significance of food and sex is, after all, survival. We cannot live without food and our children could not exist if not for sex. Nourishment is necessary to our health and well-being; the greater our health, the stronger our sexual powers. The inverse is sadly true, too.

Yet that is far from the whole story. The American sexologist, James Leslie McCary makes the above connection by saying that a well-nourished body includes 'well-nourished sexual organs capable of vigorous and continuous expression'. But McCary states precisely what this book is about when he goes on to say:

> When one has eaten a carefully prepared, subtly seasoned meal, together with wine, in an ambiance enhanced by soft music and glowing candles, one experiences a delightful glow — not only of the senses, but also of the body — a feeling that can hardly be present after one has consumed a typical American meal of meat loaf, boiled potatoes, and watery beans in a board-ing house or diner. Eating a meal of fine food is an exciting and rewarding experience for the different senses of seeing, smelling and tasting.

But what is this subtly seasoned meal in the right ambiance? We do associate various con-cepts with sex which appear in food. There is colour, shape and texture, all of which can be suggestive. All shades of red — from a tawny yellow to dark purple — are obviously more sensually arousing than a lack of colour or shades of green. Shapes which we like are obviously those which echo part of the body or the sexual organs themselves — phallic, vulva, bottom or breast-like. Textures can be crisp and hard or soft and creamy. Smells are reminiscent of skin. Herbs and spices, if they are subtle, remind us of delicate body aromas which can also make our mouths water. There is a nerve structure called Krause's end bulbs which occurs in the penis, clitoris and lips. So eating some foods is near to the act of kissing itself. Perhaps we can recall that superb scene in the film *Tom Jones*, where Albert Finney and Joyce Redman ate a meal while devouring each other with their eyes, making voluptuous love with the food, before falling into bed together. Well, I doubt whether any of the meals in this book are quite like that. Yet you, the reader, may do what you wish with the food and dishes themselves.

There is also, surrounding food, a long history of fable and myth. Many foods and spices have strong sexual connotations — spices like sage, musk, caraway, ginger, oregano, vanilla; then all types of eggs, nuts like chestnuts and walnuts, vegetables like carrots, onions, garlic, artichokes, tomatoes, potatoes and celery. In the past, potions from many of these foods were made to provoke lust and increase fertility. It is interesting to note that meat does not come into the arousal category, though steak and machismo seem to be intertwined as a contemporary myth. Oysters, of course, have always been thought of as aphrodisiac, but this is because the oyster visually can resemble the vulva.

The most famous substance of all is cantharides, known as Spanish fly. This is a beetle which, when dried and powdered, irritates the gastro-intestinal system and dilates the blood vessels. The two together, as one can imagine, would cause havoc in the genitals. The Duc de Richelieu would put Spanish fly into chocolate bonbons and feed his mistresses with them. So well known was this that the doctored sweets were called *pastilles de Richelieu*. In 1758, the dark Marquis himself, de Sade, gave a ball at Marseilles where he dosed the drinking chocolate with Spanish fly. Some say that the ball turned into an orgiastic bout, others that it just made everyone feel ill, thinking they had been poisoned. But one contemporary observer swears that women were in a 'uterine frenzy', tore off their clothes and flung themselves upon the nearest partner.

I doubt whether any of the food within this book will have that affect by itself, but in the right context, as Professor McCary has explained, food can have a most seductive effect.

Let every meal within this book have cupids attached to it.

This introduction owes much to an appendix in *Consuming Passions, a History of English Food and Appetite* by Philippa Pullar. It is she who, in this fascinating work, drew my attention to the work of J.L. McCary.

Cannelloni Verdi con Funghi e Fagioli (page 17).

January

'Love is, above all, the gift of oneself.'

Jean Anouilh, *Ardèle* (1948)

There are two flowers which I associate with this month. They are both white and their virginal purity is somewhat enticing but this, coupled with their heady scent, also makes them enigmatic. *Jasmine polyanthemum* is a climber and a greenhouse plant but its scent has a strong verbena clarity, its white sprays can easily be plucked and arranged, and it makes a perfect foil for the Christmas rose or *Helleborus niger*.

The flowers and the food decide the colours and design of the meal, which is austere black and white. Use a black tablecloth and black candles in white china sconces. Use silver cutlery, but a glass plate for the first course and white plates for the rest of the meal. The food is so highly coloured that such a table setting will show it off to its best advantage.

The first course is a French classic often used as a garnish for a steak. It is worth considering in its own right and taking a lot more trouble with it. I have both adjusted the original recipe and slightly embellished it. It should be made with fresh globe artichokes. You can, of course, use the tinned *fond d'artichaut*, but the flavour is always slightly tainted with the mineral salts from the canning. *Fond* in English means 'bottom', a word which has strong erotic associations. But artichokes have been considered since ancient times to be aphrodisiac. In the Middle Ages, in Paris, street vendors selling artichokes cried out, 'Artichokes, artichokes, heats the body and the spirit, heats the genitals.'

13

The main course may seem slightly heavy to some people, for we are eating pasta and potatoes. But the cannelloni sheets are pretty thin and Pommes Anna are delicate slivers. Besides, lovers need not eat it all. Yet I partly planned it thus because, on a cold winter evening (and this, I imagined, is a frozen and snowy January), we need warm, spicy, filling food to feel strong and lustful. Ginger has long been thought of as an aphrodisiac for, it is considered, it inflames the senses. All beans have also thought to be stimulating, I think mainly because the broad bean — the most ancient of them all — on a sideways view can resemble the female pudenda. Black beans, because of their glossy ebony colour, also radiate a certain sensuality, so the combination of black beans and ginger is famous from China to the West Indies.

You will need two large claret glasses for the dessert. Such creations look better in a large, long-stemmed glass than in a bowl where their layered beauty cannot be appreciated. This is an old English recipe, a little similar to trifle, but I have modified it with an exotic fruit from the tropics, the mango, for this is a British winter and we need the fruit, matured in the sun. Mangos are ripe when they are darkly orange and quite soft. Peel and dice the flesh on a plate so as not to lose any juice.

I would suggest a glass of well-iced Russian vodka, neat, with the first course. But have a bottle of good red Bordeaux breathing for a couple of hours before and gently adapting to the room temperature (nowhere near the fire or by the stove, though, please).

Drink a glass of Beaumes de Venise with the pudding. It may seem commonplace now, but opening a bottle of good sweet wine would be excessive and the Beaumes is astonishingly perfect with almost every dessert.

Playing quietly in the background, I have chosen Benjamin Britten's Serenade for Tenor and Horn. It is full of love arias in all possible moods.

Menu

Artichokes Montmorency

Iced Russian Vodka

Cannelloni Verdi con Funghi e
   Fagioli

Red Bordeaux

Pommes Anna

Steamed Courgettes with Parsley
   Butter

Radiccio Salad with Sesame and
   Lime Dressing and
   Dolcelatte

Tipsy Cake

Beaumes de Venise

Artichokes Montmorency

4 globe artichokes (allow 2 for each person)
2 medium carrots
1 tablespoon (15ml) minced or grated onion
2 teaspoons (10ml) walnut oil
1 teaspoon (5ml) lemon juice
1½ tablespoons (22ml) pink peppercorns
¼ pint (140ml) sour cream
Sea salt and black pepper to taste

Boil the artichokes in salted water until tender. Allow to cool. Meanwhile, take the carrots, scrape or peel them, then cut a V shape out of the top and round off the sides so that you have a long, heart shape which ends in a point on the underside. Slice across in ¼-inch (6 mm) widths. You will need 16 hearts in all, 4 for each artichoke bottom. It is a good idea to practise on a carrot or two to get the hang of the shaping. (The odds and ends can always be used for soup.) Lightly poach the 16 carrot hearts in a little salted water for about 3-4 minutes. They should still have some crunch in them.

Pluck all the leaves from the cooled artichokes and scrape off the edible bit at the base of each leaf into a bowl. Then pluck out the choke and discard. Trim the four bases or bottoms.

Mix the artichoke flesh from the leaves into a paste with the onion, walnut oil and lemon juice. Crush ½ teaspoon (2.5ml) of pink peppercorns and add that together with the sour cream and the whole pink peppercorns and seasoning.

Arrange the artichoke bottoms on two individual glass plates, add the 4 carrot hearts to each artichoke and spoon over the sauce.

Cannelloni Verdi con Funghi e Fagioli

(Green cannelloni stuffed with black beans, mushrooms and laver, covered in a paprika sauce)

4 oz (115g) dried black beans (soaked overnight)
4 sheets green cannelloni
1 oz (30g) butter
1 oz (30g) ginger root, peeled and grated
4 oz (115g) mushrooms, thinly sliced
1 small tin laver bread

For the sauce:
1 oz (30g) butter
1 oz (30g) plain flour
1 tablespoon (15ml) hot Hungarian paprika
¼ pint (140ml) milk
3 fl oz (90ml) double cream
A pinch of nutmeg
Sea salt and freshly ground black pepper

First, cook the black beans in fresh water for an hour or until they are tender. Drain and reserve.

Next, cook the cannelloni sheets in plenty of boiling, salted water for 10 minutes. Take out with a slotted spoon, place in a bowl of cold water, then drain them on a clean towel.

Melt the butter in a pan. Add the ginger and then the mushrooms. Cook gently until just tender. Add the drained beans and then the laver and continue cooking for a few minutes. Place some of the filling on each cannelloni sheet and roll up. Fit them into a buttered, shallow, ovenproof dish, join side down. Choose a size of dish that ensures they are packed closely.

Make the sauce by melting the butter, add the flour and paprika, then the milk. Cook gently before adding the cream, nutmeg and seasoning. Dribble the sauce over the top of each cannelloni so that they are partly covered.

Bake in a pre-heated oven at 400°F/200°C (Gas Mark 6) for 20 minutes.

Pommes Anna

1 lb (455g) potatoes, peeled
4 oz (115g) butter
Sea salt and black pepper

Slice the potatoes thinly in a food processor or on a mandoline. Soak them in cold water for 30 minutes, then drain, rinse and pat dry.

Butter a small, shallow, ovenproof dish. Place a layer of potatoes in the bottom, season and dot with butter. Continue with the layers until you have used up all the potatoes. Butter the top layer liberally.

Cover with a lid or foil, and bake in a pre-heated oven at 375°F/190°C (Gas Mark 5) for 30 minutes. Take out the potato cake, turn it over and return to the oven for another 30 minutes.

Raise the heat to 400°F/200°C (Gas Mark 6) so that the cannelloni can go into the oven. Bake the Pommes Anna for another 30 minutes, then pour off all the butter before serving and leave to brown a little, uncovered, in the warm oven.

Steamed Courgettes with Parsley Butter

1½ oz (40g) softened butter
Generous handful of parsley, finely chopped
Sea salt and freshly ground black pepper
4 small courgettes, washed and trimmed

A few hours before cooking the courgettes, cream the butter with the parsley, season and refrigerate.

Slice the courgettes lengthways to the top but leave about half an inch (12 mm) of the top whole. Steam them for 5 minutes. Arrange on a dish in a fan shape. Melt the parsley butter and pour over.

Radiccio Salad with Sesame and Lime Dressing with Dolcelatte

If you have managed to get a piece of Dolcelatte at its peak, thus soft, creamy and just about to run, make now a sharp radiccio salad — merely a few leaves — and dress it with a sprinkling of sesame oil and a squeeze of lime juice and eat both together to cleanse and stimulate the palate. Finish the wine between you and make this modest course last.

Tipsy Cake

A little sponge cake, or 6 sponge fingers, broken and crumbled
1 tablespoon (15ml) brandy
2 teaspoons (10ml) dry sherry
¼ pint (140ml) double cream
2 tablespoons (30ml) castor sugar
2 egg yolks
1 ripe mango
2 tablespoons (30ml) toasted almonds

Divide the sponge at the bottom of the glasses and pour over the brandy and sherry. Leave for an hour.

Meanwhile, make the custard. Put the cream in a double boiler, add 1 tablespoon (15ml) of sugar and stir in the egg yolks. Heat gently until the cream thickens. Peel and dice the mango and add it to the two glasses. Sprinkle the fruit with the remaining tablespoon (15ml) of castor sugar. Add the custard, pouring carefully. Sprinkle the almonds on top and refrigerate for a few hours.

Chestnut and Cabbage Mould (page 25).

February

'To fall in love is to create a religion that has a
fallible god.'

Jorge Luis Borges, 'The Meeting in a Dream',
Other Inquisitions (1952)

This month celebrates St Valentine's Day which lovers enjoy. The Christian saint has
little to do with this day of romance. There was a vague idea that birds began to mate
upon the 14th of February, so this example was hastily echoed among humankind. I
personally believe that lovers don't need any excuse and that Valentine's Day can be any
day you want to make it.

In this month, the first sprigs of forsythia are about to bloom in the garden. Pick
some and arrange them — their tiny yellow flowers are a sign of the closeness of spring.
Dine from a highly polished table, then the flowers and candlelight are reflected in it. Play
Mozart softly in the background — a piano or flute concerto, perhaps.

We all know the beautiful colour of beetroot soup or borscht, but an even more
stunning hue can be obtained from beetroot if it is transparent. The flavour is just as good.
The transparency of the soup, which is made into a jelly, is achieved by not blending the
vegetable with the stock but by leaching out all its goodness and then throwing away the
vegetable debris.

You can buy tofu smoked and it can be cut into any shape you like. Make the *coeur*
from a heart-shaped ramekin.

The Elizabethans believed that chestnuts stimulated lust because they were flatulent.

21

We possibly find this association odd if not comical. Buttes in his *Dyets Dry Dinner*, thought the nut 'resembleth testes, the instrument of lust'. Both walnuts and chestnuts go well with the winter green vegetables, whether they stimulate lust or not, and this mould celebrates that fusion with the addition of a little sage. It is a traditionally Lenten and English dish, although it would then have been covered with a pastry crust rather than the blanched cabbage leaves. In contrast to this, the okra or lady's-fingers are cooked in an Eastern spicy sauce. To complete the main course, what could be more satisfactory than potato balls.

Chocolate has many strong associations with love. Madame du Barry gave chocolate to all her lovers. Casanova drank it instead of champagne. A German eighteenth-century copperplate shows a young wife offering a cup of chocolate to her octogenarian husband with the words, 'Drink, my love, for we must still give heirs to the waiting world.'

To drink before the meal, try Kir, that combination of white wine and Crème de cassis. Then with the first course, just drink the wine itself. I suggest a Sauvignon Blanc with its crisp but slightly smoky aroma. The main course with cabbage and chestnuts can stand a robust red wine like a Valpolicella or a Hungarian Pinot Noir. This will stand up to the Roquefort which follows. Chocolate swamps all wines, so I would wait and drink a good Armagnac afterwards.

Menu

Coeurs de Betterave au Feuilles
   du Tofu Fumé   Sauvignon Blanc

Chestnut and Cabbage Mould   Valpolicella *or*
Spiced Okra   Hungarian Pinot Noir
Potato Balls

Roquefort and Batavia Salad

Petit Pots Chocolat Menthe

Coeurs de Betterave au Feuilles du Tofu Fumé

1 lb (455g) raw beetroot, peeled and grated
2 onions, chopped
5 cloves garlic, peeled and chopped
1 oz (30g) ginger root, peeled and grated
1½ pints (850ml) water
Seasoning
1 sachet vegetarian gelatine or
2 teaspoons (10ml) agar-agar
1 × ½ lb (225g) packet smoked tofu
1 small courgette for garnish

Place the beetroot, onions, garlic and ginger in an ovenproof dish or casserole. Add the water and a little seasoning, give the mixture a stir and bring to the boil. Cook in a pre-heated oven at 350°F/180°C (Gas Mark 4) for 2½ hours. Allow to cool, then pour off the clear liquid. Taste and season again if necessary.

Melt the gelatine in some of the liquid; or melt the agar-agar in some of the liquid but simmer for 5 minutes. Return the liquid to the rest of the stock. Give a good and thorough stir, then fill two heart-shaped ramekins with the liquid. Refrigerate for 24 hours.

To assemble, cut 4 thin leaf shapes from the tofu. Cut a 1-inch (24mm) chunk from the courgette, then cut the green skin pieces into julienne strips. Turn out the heart-shaped jelly onto a white plate. Decorate each side with two of the leaves and place the courgette 'stalks' splayed out at the bottom.

Chestnut and Cabbage Mould

Use a 2½ pint (1.5 litre) soufflé dish.

1 medium size Savoy cabbage
6 oz (170g) dried chestnuts (soaked overnight)
2 oz (55g) butter
1 teaspoon (5ml) dried sage
Sea salt and freshly ground black pepper
3 eggs, beaten
¼ pint (140ml) double cream

Take all the large outside leaves from the cabbage. Place them in a bowl and pour boiling water over, then leave for 5 minutes. Bring the chestnuts to the boil and simmer for 30 minutes. Leave to cool, then peel off all bits of brown skin which tend to stick in the crevices and chop the nuts coarsely. Chop the rest of the cabbage. Melt the butter in a pan and cook the cabbage and sage in it until the cabbage is just soft but still *al dente*. Stir in the nuts and seasoning. When it has cooled down a little, mix in the eggs and cream.

Butter the soufflé dish and arrange the blanched cabbage leaves so that they line the bottom and sides, leaving enough overhang for the top. Pour in the mixture to reach almost to the top. Cover with the leaves.

Place buttered paper over the top and place the dish in a *bain-marie* in a preheated oven at 400°F/200°C (Gas Mark 6) for 40 minutes. Take from the oven and test the centre with a knife. If it comes out clean, it is done. If not place back in the oven for another 10 minutes. When the mould is cooked, let it rest for 10 minutes before unmoulding onto a platter.

Spiced Okra

½ lb (225g) okra
3 tablespoons (45ml) corn oil
1 teaspoon (5ml) each mustard seeds and whole fenugreek
1 red chilli, broken
1 teaspoon (5ml) cardamom, crushed
½ teaspoon (2.5ml) each cumin and coriander
¼ pint (140ml) water
2 tablespoons (30ml) shoyu sauce
1 oz (30g) creamed coconut, grated

Wash and trim the okra. Heat the oil in a pan and throw in all the spices. Sauté for a few minutes until the mustard seeds pop. Lower the heat and do not let them burn. Throw in the okra. Stir for a moment, then add the water. Simmer over a low heat for 15 minutes. Add the shoyu and then the coconut. The minute it has thickened, take from the heat. If it is too thick and gungy, add a little more water and shoyu.

Potato Balls

1½ lb (680g) potatoes, peeled
1 oz (30g) butter
2 egg yolks
1 egg, beaten
Breadcrumbs for coating
Oil for frying

Boil the potatoes, then mash and push them through a sieve. Mix in the butter, together with the egg yolks. Shape into balls, dip into beaten egg, then roll in breadcrumbs. Fry until brown and crisp on the outside.

Roquefort and Batavia Salad

Batavia is slightly sharp and bitter, and its leaves in the centre are a glowing lime green. Use some of these central leaves with a little darker green leaf from the outside. Dice about 2 oz (55g) of Roquefort and throw it onto the leaves. Sprinkle with a little olive oil and red wine vinegar, a little sea salt and black pepper. Toss thoroughly and enjoy it.

Petit Pots Chocolat Menthe

4 oz (115g) dark bitter chocolate
1 tablespoon (15ml) Crème de menthe
¼ pint (140ml) double cream
A pinch of salt
1 egg, beaten
2 drops vanilla essence

Break the chocolate into a blender jar and reduce to a grated consistency. Add the Crème de menthe to the cream in a double boiler and, before it boils, pour onto the chocolate, adding the salt, egg and vanilla essence. Blend to a smooth, thick cream. Pour into two ramekins and refrigerate for a day.

Pickled Cabbage and Caerphilly (page 35).

March

'Love, with very young people, is a heartless business. We drink at that age from thirst, or to get drunk; it is only later in life that we occupy ourselves with the individuality of our wine.'

Isak Dinesen, 'The Old Chevalier',
Seven Gothic Tales (1934)

March celebrates St David and St Patrick, so why not a meal which echoes Wales and Ireland? Fill vases with daffodils, narcissi and jonquils and celebrate spring as well. Choose a table setting in white, yellow and green so that you are carrying through the spring colours.

There is little, possibly, in the first course which seems to stem from either country. But nori, or laver, is a seaweed and the poor of Wales and Ireland have used seaweeds wisely since ancient times as a staple part of their diet. Nori is the Japanese form of laver and you can buy it in sheets which have been dried and roasted. There is no need to cook it, though you can place it beneath a grill where it will turn brittle and green and then crumble it over food, using it as a condiment. Here, and in other dishes, I have used it to wrap around food like a leaf but, unlike leaves, nori sheets do not have to be blanched; they can be merely moistened, dipped in a solution of water and shoyu sauce. They are then pliable.

Both the Anglesey Eggs and the Pease Pudding are Welsh dishes, though the former uses a mixture of potato and leek which is a little reminiscent of Colcannon, that marvellous Irish dish of mashed potato, spring onions and other greens (whatever is at hand — even kale). So I believe this dish stems in its feeling from both countries. Pease pudding, too, is beloved by both the Welsh and the Irish and, heavens above, is loved by anyone who tastes it. How absurd for the trendy cooks or gourmet restaurants to ignore such good food as this. Pease pudding, in my view, deserves to belong in the hierarchy of great dishes. Yet it is simplicity to make.

Instead of a leaf salad, I have used cabbage and pickled it in a way which belongs, I admit, to the Far East. But why not? So many spiced dishes have come from there and been incorporated as part of the British cuisine. This one, too, deserves a place there. Its heat, I believe, goes beautifully with a mature, farmhouse Caerphilly.

Drink with this meal an excellent white wine — like a Chablis Premier Cru. Follow with a Portuguese Dão or a red Rioja. The rhubarb fool will happily take a dessert wine and why not one of the most fragrant, a Monbazillac.

Menu

Nori Ring Mould, with Green
    Peppered Avocado Purée and
    Tomato Sauce

Chablis Premier Cru

Anglesey Eggs
Pease Pudding

Portuguese Dão *or*
    Red Rioja

Pickled Cabbage
Caerphilly

Spiced Rhubarb Fool

Monbazillac

Nori Ring Mould with Green Peppered Avocado Purée and Tomato Sauce

2 nori sheets
1 tablespoon (15ml) shoyu sauce
1 tablespoon (15ml) water
4 Petit Suisse cheeses or
2 oz (55g) cream cheese
3 spring onions, finely chopped
1 small potato, boiled and mashed
1 oz (30g) butter, softened
Sea salt and black pepper

For the avocado purée:

1 ripe avocado
2 tablespoons (30ml) sour cream
Sea salt and black pepper
2 teaspoons (10ml) green peppercorns

For the tomato sauce:

1 lb (455g) ripe tomatoes
3 fl oz (90ml) sherry
Sea salt and black pepper

Use two individual ring moulds. Cut the nori sheets in half, moisten them in the shoyu and water for a moment. Arrange each half around the moulds, leaving some overhang. Mix all the other ingredients together thoroughly. Place in each mould and fold over the nori, smoothing it down with your fingers. Refrigerate for a few hours.

To make the purée, simply blend the avocado flesh with the cream and seasoning. Stir in the green peppercorns.

For the tomato sauce, cook the tomatoes with the sherry over a low heat so that they simmer in their own juice. Add the seasoning, then push them through a sieve. If the sauce seems too thin, reduce over a flame.

To assemble the dish, with a knife ease out the ring moulds onto individual plates. Pile the centre with the avocado purée, then dribble the red tomato sauce around the outside of the mould.

Anglesey Eggs

1 lb (455g) leeks, washed and finely chopped
1 oz (30g) butter
1 lb (455g) potatoes, peeled and boiled
Sea salt and freshly ground black pepper
2 oz (55g) cream cheese
3 eggs, hard-boiled

For the sauce:

1 oz (30g) butter
1 oz (30g) flour
½ pint (285ml) single cream
Sea salt and freshly ground black pepper
2 oz (55g) mature Cheddar, grated

Cook the leeks in the butter until tender. Mash the drained potatoes. Combine the leeks and potato with seasoning and the cream cheese. Peel and quarter the eggs.

Make the sauce by making a roux with the butter and flour, the cream, seasoning and cheese, and stir until smooth.

Choose a shallow ovenproof dish. Pile up the potato and cheese mixture around the sides. Place the eggs in the centre. Pour the cheese sauce over the eggs and bake in a preheated oven at 400°F/200°C (Gas Mark 6) for 20 minutes or until just brown.

Pease Pudding

½ lb (225g) split peas (soaked overnight)
1 egg, beaten
1 oz (30g) butter
Sea salt and freshly ground black pepper

Place the soaked peas in a muslin bag and boil for about 1 hour, adding a little salt.

When the peas are tender, take them out and blend them with the egg, butter and seasoning — use plenty of freshly ground black pepper.

Pour into a buttered ovenproof dish and place in a hot oven at 400°F/200°C (Gas Mark 6) for 20 minutes — it can go beneath the Anglesey Eggs.

Pickled Cabbage

Make this dish the day before. However, it will keep happily, covered, in the refrigerator for a week if need be.

1 small white cabbage, grated
1 teaspoon (5ml) sea salt
2 teaspoons (10ml) castor sugar
2 tablespoons (30ml) sesame oil
½ oz (15g) ginger root, grated
1 dried red chilli, broken
1 teaspoon (5ml) white and black peppercorns, roughly crushed
3 fl oz (90ml) dry vermouth

Place the grated cabbage in a bowl and sprinkle with the salt. Leave for 1 hour, then squeeze all the moisture out of it. Transfer to a clean bowl and sprinkle with the sugar.

Heat the oil and throw in the ginger and chilli. Sauté the spices for a moment or two, then pour the hot oil and spices over the cabbage. Stir thoroughly, then mix in the peppercorns and vermouth. Refrigerate for a day.

Serve with a moist and mature Caerphilly.

Spiced Rhubarb Fool

½ lb (225g) rhubarb
1 tablespoon (15ml) castor sugar
½ teaspoon (2.5ml) allspice
A pinch of cinnamon
¼ pint (140ml) double cream

Slice the rhubarb and place over a low heat in a pan with the sugar and spices. Cook until just tender. Leave to cool, then blend with the cream. Pour into tall glasses and serve with *langues de chat*.

*Tarte Courdiform de Poireaux (page 41) and
Croquettes de Pommes de Terre aux Herbes
Fines (page 41).*

'Love is sweet, but tastes best with bread.'

Yiddish proverb (1949)

April and spring turn the thoughts inevitably to Paris. This then is a stylish French meal, far more stylish than the French could possibly create, for it is without meat. But let us eat it in a French setting, on a balcony, by candlelight, within sight and sound of the Seine and Piaf or Asnavour in the background, or perhaps Bizet or Debussy by the time you have reached the dessert (though you should not forget Rossini to go with the salad). Gay lovers should always recall Bizet's duet from *The Pearl Fishers*, one of the great romantic arias in the repertoire — enough passion there to whip the egg whites stiff. Decorate the table with sprigs of cherry blossom.

This, too, is the month when we can buy the first green asparagus and how good it is with this light *beurre fondue*. Asparagus was enjoyed by the Ancient World. It is part of the lily family but unique in that it has no leaves. The stem which we eat is particularly sensitive to sunlight, producing a food rich in nutrients. So it is not only the shape that delights a romantic heart but also its purpose.

The Romans distributed the leek from the Mediterranean throughout their Empire. From earliest times, this vegetable had a reputation as an aphrodisiac which Chaucer alludes to as a nostalgic memory in the old:

'wanted a hoary head and a green tail like leeks . . .
What we can't do no more we talk about and make the ashes when the
fire is out.'

Luckily for lovers, you can buy heart-shaped pie tins in all sizes, and this is a small tart for two so that the whole heart is consumed at the one sitting. There is something overtly romantic in eating every crumb when it appears to be a symbol of present love. As to the vegetables which complement the heart, they are unashamedly phallic though modestly small for most appetites, but how good they are just to nibble.

The salad is as light, cheerful and charming as the music after which the dish is named. The cheese I have chosen to go with the salad is a Gaperon, slightly flavoured with pink garlic from the Auvergne. Its shape is as appealing as its flavour.

Peaches are definitely female and were revered by the ancients as an erotic fruit. Here they are stuffed with dark red cherries and quickly baked in the oven.

Muscadet is a popular dry wine and the one I have suggested is the best, having a peachy quality — good with the asparagus. Côtes du Roussillon is a light fruity wine which comes from a part of southern France between Provence and the Pyrenées and has become more widely known in recent times. Marsala has a highly distinctive flavour and is a very good alternative to Madeira, being darker and stronger in taste. It goes excellently with fruit.

Menu

Les Asperges au Beurre Fondue   Muscadet de Sèvre et
  (Asparagus with lemon butter)   Maine

Tarte Courdiform de Poireaux   Côtes du Roussillon
  (Heart-shaped leek tart)
Croquettes de Pommes de Terre
  aux Herbes Fines
  (Herb potato croquettes)
Les Carottes en Eau de Rose
  (Carrots in rose water)

Salad Rossini
Gaperon

Les Pêches Farcis aux Cerises   Marsala
  (Stuffed peaches with cherries)

Les Asperges au Beurre Fondue

1 lb (455g) asparagus spears
3 oz (85g) butter
2 tablespoons (30ml) lemon juice
1 tablespoon (15ml) water
Pinch of cayenne pepper

Trim the asparagus and steam it for 8-12 minutes. Meanwhile, melt 2 oz (55g) of the butter, add the lemon juice, water and cayenne. Beat with a whisk and slowly add the rest of the butter until you have a frothy emulsion. Pour into a jug to serve.

If you are fortunate enough to have asparagus plates, decorated with the vegetable and with a receptacle at the centre for the sauce, use them. If not, angle a plate so that it is lower at the inside, so that the sauce stops in one place — easier to dip the tips of the asparagus into.

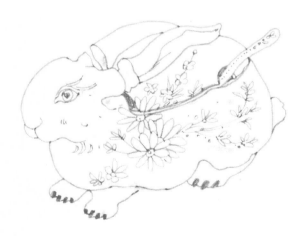

Tarte Courdiform de Poireaux

6 oz (170g) shortcrust pastry
1 lb (455g) leeks, trimmed and sliced
1 oz (30g) butter
5 oz (140g) fromage frais
2 oz (55g) Gruyère, grated
Sea salt and freshly ground black pepper

Roll out the pastry and line the heart-shaped tin. Cover with beans and bake blind.

Cook the leeks slowly in the butter with a little salt and pepper until they are soft, about 8-10 minutes. Turn out into a mixing bowl and add the *fromage frais* and Gruyère. Mix well, pour into the pastry case and bake in a pre-heated oven at 400°F/200°C (Gas Mark 6) for 20 minutes or until the top is golden brown. Take from the oven. Leave to cool for 10 minutes and serve warm.

Croquettes de Pommes de Terre aux Herbes Fines

1 lb (455g) potatoes, peeled and boiled
2 eggs, beaten separately
3 tablespoons (45ml) each finely chopped parsley, chives and mint
Sea salt and freshly ground black pepper
Flour
Breadcrumbs
Corn oil for frying

Mash the potatoes to a smooth purée. Add one beaten egg, all the herbs and the seasoning. Roll into small sausage shapes. Refrigerate for an hour, then dip each croquette into a little flour, then the remaining beaten egg and then the breadcrumbs.

Fry in a little corn oil until crisp and brown.

Les Carottes en Eau de Rose

1 lb (455g) baby carrots
4 tablespoons (60ml) water
2 tablespoons (30ml) rose water
2 oz (55g) butter
Sea salt and freshly ground black pepper

Trim and scrape the carrots. Mix the water, rose water, butter and seasoning together in a pan. Bring to the boil. Throw the carrots in and simmer for 15 minutes. Drain and serve.

Salad Rossini

1 small cos lettuce
1 small celery heart
5 or 6 young dandelion leaves
½ bunch watercress
1 tablespoon (15ml) lemon juice
3 tablespoons (45ml) hazelnut oil
Sea salt and freshly ground black pepper

Slice the lettuce, celery and dandelion leaves into julienne strips, and chop the watercress small. Place in a salad bowl. Mix the vinaigrette ingredients together and, just before serving, pour over the salad and toss well.

Slice the Gaperon like a cake in small wedges to eat with the salad.

Les Pêches Farcis aux Cerises

2 ripe peaches
½ lb (225g) dark red cherries
1 tablespoon (15ml) castor sugar
1 oz (30g) butter, softened
3 fl oz (90ml) Beaumes de Venise (or similar white dessert wine)

Slice the peaches in half and extract the stones. Stone the cherries but keep them as whole as you can. Place in a bowl with the sugar and butter. Mix well. Fill the peach cavities with the mixture. Place the four halves in an oven dish, pour the Beaumes de Venise over and bake in a pre-heated oven at 400°F/200°C (Gas Mark 6) for 10 minutes. Serve with a good dollop of whipped cream.

Pawpaw and Pomegranate Fruit Salad (page 51).

May

'Love is a spirit all compact of fire.'

Shakespeare, *Venus and Adonis* (1593)

May mornings we associate with Oxford, spring and punting on the river; the May Balls of Cambridge, too.

'In youth is pleasure': Denton Welch used the phrase for one of his novels. The spring of the year reflects this instinctive urging towards new life, in which romance and love play their inevitable part.

Shades of pink are particularly flattering. Such a colour is, of course, reminiscent of flesh but the colour is reflected also in so many spring flowers. A room or table for May, decorated with pink lilac, would have a strong perfume and look beautiful. The flower lasts much longer if you strip it of leaves. It also arranges itself better in a bowl. Continue the colour scheme in the place settings. And play Puccini softly in the background — Puccini, the most romantic of all opera composers, distils the essence of an emotion in the arias that his sopranos sing.

Fragrant soups can be mysterious and seductive and lovage is one of the most fragrant of all herbs — reminiscent of celery, only stronger. It has a long and honourable history of being a stimulant to the senses.

I make no apologies for using asparagus again in this month as it is a vegetable of supreme delight and, while its season continues, lovers should enjoy every mouthful.

In this month, the first rocket should be growing, and its leaves can be picked for salad. This was one of the salads named by the Romans as inducing lechery. In the Middle

Ages, monks were forbidden to grow rocket in the monastery gardens as it was thought to be such a powerful aphrodisiac. Yet the monks grew it in secret and we must be grateful that they did for the plant might have vanished for ever if they had not.

The Fourme d'Ambert is one of the oldest of all the blue cheeses and it goes particularly well with the rocket. It needs a robust red wine. The Bulgarian Cabernet I've chosen for the dessert goes equally well, I believe, with the blue cheese and the slightly abrasive fruitiness of the pomegranate in the fruit salad.

Pomegranates are beautiful. The seeds are eaten enclosed in tiny translucent beads of pink and purple flesh, like the tears of some remote goddess. In the Ancient World, the pomegranate appeared as a symbol of fertility on the robes of emperors and rulers, built into architecture, decorating gateways and porches. When Persephone was snatched and kept by Pluto in the Underworld, she made the mistake of eating six pomegranate seeds and thus caused the six chill months of winter.

There is a nasty little Greek legend which explains the circlet at the top of this fruit. A young girl believed she was destined to wear a crown. Bacchus fell in love with her and promised her one. The silly girl believed him, and instead of saving herself for a prince, she gave herself to a god and was changed immediately into a pomegranate tree.

To go with the intense, herby flavour of the lovage, you will need a crisp, dry, fortified wine. Choose the best Spanish sherry that you can afford. Follow it with an Alsace Pinot which is again very dry but with a hint of fruitiness. It will cut across the soufflé and spinach in black butter. Enjoy with the pudding the heartiness of a strong red Bulgarian Cabernet.

Menu

Cream of Lovage Soup   Dry Sherry

Asparagus Soufflé   Alsace Pinot
New Potatoes
Spinach Beurre Noir

Rocket Salad
Fourme d'Ambert

Pawpaw and Pomegranate   Bulgarian Cabernet
  Fruit Salad

Cream of Lovage Soup

2 oz (55g) butter
3 tablespoons (45ml) finely chopped lovage
1 onion, finely chopped
3 cloves garlic, crushed
4 oz (115g) potatoes, peeled and boiled
Seasoning
1 pint (570ml) vegetable stock
¼ pint (140ml) single cream

Melt the butter in a pan, add the lovage, onion, garlic and potatoes. Sweat in the butter for a few minutes before adding the seasoning and stock. Bring to the boil and simmer for 15 minutes. Leave to cool, then blend to a smooth consistency. Reheat gently, adding the cream, and sprinkle a little more finely chopped lovage over the surface.

Asparagus Soufflé

A soufflé is not at all difficult to make — it just has to be timed exactly. A soufflé of four eggs in a 2½-pint (1.5 litre) soufflé dish placed in a pre-heated oven at 425°F/220°C (Gas Mark 7), will be cooked in 20 minutes — that is, the top will have risen and be brown, while the centre is runny.

1 lb (455g) asparagus
4 eggs, separated
2 oz (55g) Gruyère cheese, grated
Sea salt and black pepper
1 oz (30g) butter
1 oz (30g) flour
½ pint (285ml) single cream

Cook the asparagus in a little salted water for 8 minutes or until tender. Cut it into chunks and place in a mixing bowl with the egg yolks, Gruyère and seasoning. Mix roughly.

Melt the butter in a pan and add the flour. Make a roux, then add the cream. Stir gently to get a smooth sauce. Remove from the heat and allow to cool.

Whip the egg whites until stiff. Pour the cooled sauce over the asparagus mixture and mix thoroughly. Then fold in the whites. Pour into a soufflé dish which has been well buttered. Place in a pre-heated oven and cook for 20 minutes.

New Potatoes

Use plenty of mint with the potatoes, boiling or steaming them with their skins on. When done, toss them in a little butter and sour cream.

Spinach Beurre Noir

1 lb (455g) spinach leaves
2 oz (55g) butter
Juice of 1 lemon
½ tablespoon (8ml) coarsely crushed black peppercorns
A pinch each of nutmeg and salt

Wash the spinach and drain very carefully.

    Melt the butter in a pan and add the lemon juice and crushed peppercorns. Throw in the spinach. Add the nutmeg and salt, give the mixture a stir. Leave to simmer over a gentle heat for 5 minutes until the spinach is done.

Rocket Salad

1 tablespoon (15ml) red wine vinegar
1 clove garlic, crushed
1 tablespoon (15ml) Dijon mustard
4 tablespoons (60ml) olive oil
Sea salt and black pepper
1 small heart of lettuce
A generous bunch of rocket leaves

Mix the vinaigrette ingredients thoroughly and let it stand. In a bowl, arrange the lettuce leaves. Chop the rocket leaves small and scatter over the lettuce heart. Toss the salad with some of the dressing at the table before serving with the Fourme d'Ambert.

Pawpaw and Pomegranate Fruit Salad

2 ripe pawpaw
1 ripe pomegranate
1 tablespoon (15ml) castor sugar

Cut the pawpaw in half and scoop out the seeds. Peel, then thinly slice the flesh into a bowl.

Cut the pomegranate in half and scoop out the seeds. Scatter them over the pawpaw and sprinkle with castor sugar.

Leave for a few hours in the refrigerator before serving.

Dolmades of Lettuce and Curd Cheese (page 56).

Now is the beginning of summer, with so much flowering and fruiting in the garden. Fill the room you'll dine in with the scent of honeysuckle and freesias and undercut that aroma with the earthy and sensual voice of Ella Fitzgerald singing Cole Porter. The colours of early summer are so vibrant that the place setting should be cool and white.

There is always something undeniably sexy about small parcels of food which have to be unwrapped. They are like gifts and there is an element of surprise in what they enwrap.

June is a good month for the first broad beans. This delicious pulse was the bean grown and eaten by the Ancient Greeks. It was even used as currency. Pythagoras told his pupils not to consume it and no one has decided exactly why, though some believe that it was because the Greeks believed that beans contained the souls of the dead. My own theory is that a side view of the bean resembles the female pudenda; thus it was thought sacred and a symbol of fertility. The childless were encouraged to eat beans so as to increase desire and fertility.

The casserole given here is made from three different beans, cabbage and spiced with coriander in a cream and white wine sauce. To accompany this is a millet pilaf flavoured with red pepper and chilli. Both the salad and the dessert are globe shaped to remind one of the female principle. The cheese, Saint-Nectaire, is a pressed, firm, yellow cheese of delicate but decisive flavour — a perfect foil to the fruit in both salad and dessert.

To go with these delicate dolmades, have one of the best wines for lovers. The grape this wine comes from is called Blanc Fumé which refers to the heavily smoky aroma in the bouquet. This grape also produces marvellous white wines in both California and New Zealand. The best of the Sauvignon blancs can be quite aromatic but most also have a hint of this smoky scent.

With the main course, choose a Savigny which is a light but fruity wine and will not overload the digestion. A good vintage port is superb with Charentais melon.

Menu

Dolmades of Lettuce and
   Curd Cheese

Sauvignon Blanc

Three-Bean Casserole in a
   White Wine Sauce
Millet Pilaf with Red Pepper
   and Chilli

Savigny (or a light
   youngish red wine)

Salad Imperatrice
Saint-Nectaire

Charentais Melon Stuffed
   with Strawberries

Vintage Port ('55, '60
   or '66)

Dolmades of Lettuce and Curd Cheese

6 lettuce leaves
5 oz (140g) curd cheese
½ bunch spring onions, finely chopped
1 oz (30g) butter, softened
1 tablespoon (15ml) green peppercorns
2 tablespoons (30ml) parsley, finely chopped
Sea salt and black pepper

Blanch the lettuce leaves by pouring boiling water over them, then drain in a colander. Mix all the other ingredients together. Place a heaped tablespoon at one end of the lettuce leaf and roll up gently, folding in the sides, so that you have a neat package. Continue with all six and refrigerate for half a day.

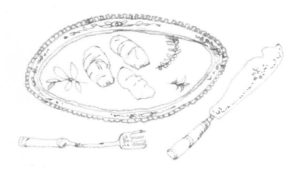

Three-Bean Casserole in a White Wine Sauce

4 oz (115g) flageolet beans, soaked overnight
½ lb (225g) broad beans, podded
½ lb (225g) French beans, sliced
2 oz (55g) butter
1 teaspoon (5ml) coriander, roughly crushed
2 cloves garlic, crushed
½ small cabbage, thinly sliced
1 oz (30g) flour
½ pint (285ml) dry white wine
Sea salt and black pepper
½ pint (285ml) single cream

Cook the flageolet beans in water, covering them by half an inch. Simmer gently and watch that they do not dry out. They should be tender in 30-40 minutes. Add the broad and French beans and cook for a further 10 minutes.

Meanwhile, melt the butter in a casserole and add the coriander and garlic. Throw in the cabbage and cook for a few minutes or until just soft. Sprinkle in the flour and cook for a few more minutes. Then add the wine, bring to the boil and simmer for a few more minutes. Drain the beans and add them to the casserole. Season and cook for another moment. Finally, add the cream and bring back to just below boiling point. Simmer for 5 minutes, then serve.

The casserole can be made and left for an hour, then carefully reheated.

Millet Pilaf with Red Pepper and Chilli

4 oz (115g) millet
2 tablespoons (30ml) olive oil
1 dried red chilli, broken
1 red pepper, cored, seeded and sliced
Sea salt and black pepper
1 tablespoon (15ml) pink peppercorns

Pour boiling water over the millet to cover and simmer for 15 minutes, by which time the millet should have absorbed all the water.

Meanwhile, heat the olive oil. Throw in the broken red chilli and the pepper. Fry briskly for 5 minutes. When the millet is done, add the chillied pepper and juices. Stir in, season and scatter with a few pink peppercorns.

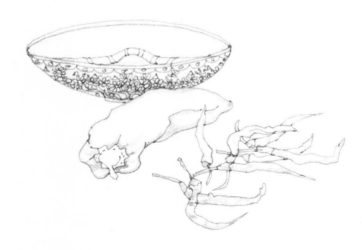

Salad Imperatrice

1 large orange
1 tablespoon (15ml) whisky
1 tablespoon (15ml) sour cream
Sea salt and freshly ground pepper
A few cos lettuce leaves
A few radishes
A few spring onions
A few stalks of celery

Cut the orange in half and scoop out all the flesh. Remove the pith and seeds and chop the flesh. Place in a large bowl with the whisky and sour cream. Season well.

Chop and slice the remaining ingredients into julienne strips. Add to the orange and toss thoroughly. Pile into the two empty orange shells.

Cut the Saint-Nectaire like a cake. Peel the cheese and eat thin wedges with the salad.

Charentais Melon Stuffed with Strawberries

2 small Charentais melons
½ lb (225g) strawberries
2 tablespoons (30ml) castor sugar

Cut the top third from the melons and scoop out all the seeds. Drain or drink the juice.

Hull and halve or quarter the strawberries. Pile them into the melon cavity, sprinkle sugar on top and refrigerate for a few hours.

Chilled Avocado and Mint Soup (page 64).

July

'Love consists in this, that two solitudes protect
and border and salute each other.'

Rainer Maria Rilke, *Letters to a Young Poet*,
14 May, 1904
(tr. M.D. Herter Norton)

This is a cool meal planned for a late summer evening, designed to be eaten out of doors, in the garden by lamplight. One can now buy flares which are stuck in the earth and will flicker and remain alight in the breeze. The lighting is important, so take trouble with positioning, hiding lamps discreetly and cunningly behind foliage and in trees so that they will shed a gentle and lambent glow upon the table. As midges and mosquitos can be a nuisance even in our cold clime, it would be well to install an anti-midge device, or spray the table and environs with a repellent about fifteen minutes before eating. There are now many small terracotta urns and carvings which will take slow-burning candles. Keep the table setting plain and simple. Use the best silver, cutlery and glass, for the light makes such things look even more beautiful. Use as background music something serene like Albinoni, Pachelbel or other composers of the Baroque style.

Though the meal is a cold one, it is subtly spiced with many of the herbs thought to be stimulating to romance. Avocado makes the most beautiful cold soup of all, but in the summer, it is good to have it flavoured with mint.

The three-tiered mould of the main course has ginger with the laver and a hint of caraway with the cauliflower. The cheese is the richest of the blue cheeses, the Italian

Dolcelatte. And the dessert would seduce an ice goddess, it looks and tastes so enchanting — alternating strips of red and white currants beneath a glaze of quince jelly.

An excellent aperitif and a particularly good accompaniment to the soup is Pineau des Charentes, which is a mixture of Cognac and fresh grape juice. To follow, choose a Meursault which is one of the great white wines, a dry golden and mellow wine. To go with the tart, choose a good quality, sweet sherry from Spain.

Menu

Chilled Avocado and Mint
  Soup

Pineau des Charentes

Three-tiered Mould
Stuffed Peppers

Meursault

Mixed Leaf Salad with
  Dolcelatte

Glazed White and Red
  Currant Tart

Vouvray

Chilled Avocado and Mint Soup

1 ripe avocado
1 clove garlic, crushed
3 tablespoons (45ml) freshly chopped mint
Sea salt and black pepper
12 fl oz (340ml) milk

Place the flesh of the avocado into a blender jar. Add the garlic, mint, seasoning and milk. Process until smooth and creamy. Refrigerate for a few hours.

Three-tiered Mould

1 lb (455g) carrots
1 small cauliflower
1 oz (30g) butter
1 oz (30g) ginger root, grated
1 small tin laver
3 eggs, beaten separately
Sea salt and black pepper
½ pint (285ml) single cream
A pinch of caraway

Trim and scrape the carrots. Boil them in salted water. Slice the cauliflower into pieces and steam them over the carrots. Heat the butter in a pan and sauté the ginger root for a few minutes. Take away from the heat and mix in the laver.

When the vegetables are tender, drain them carefully. Place the carrots in a blender with one beaten egg and seasoning. Blend to a thick purée. Add a third of the cream and blend again. Butter a 2½-pint (1.5 litre) soufflé dish and pour in the carrot purée.

Stir one beaten egg and a third of the cream into the laver purée. Pour that carefully over the carrot.

Now blend the cauliflower with the remaining egg, the rest of the cream and a pinch of caraway. Season and pour over the laver.

Cover with buttered paper, place in a *bain-marie* and cook in a pre-heated oven at 425°F/220°C (Gas Mark 7) for 30 minutes or until a knife inserted in the centre comes out clean. Leave for 20 minutes before unmoulding onto a platter.

Stuffed Peppers

3 oz (85g) Patna rice
½ lb (225g) fresh garden peas, podded
3 shallots, finely sliced
Sea salt and black pepper
2 medium-sized green peppers, cored and seeded (tops reserved)
¼ pint (140ml) dry white wine

Boil the rice with the peas and shallots until just tender. Drain thoroughly and season. Fill the peppers with the mixture and cover with the pepper tops.

Choose a saucepan which just holds the two peppers so that they remain upright. Pour the wine around them, season, bring to the boil and simmer for 15 minutes. Turn the heat off and let them stand in the pan until quite cold.

Drain and place on a serving platter.

Mixed Leaf Salad with Dolcelatte

In high summer, there is every imaginable leaf available — radiccio, rocket, endive, chicory. From the garden, there are nasturtium and dandelion leaves; there are flowers like marigolds, daisies and rose petals. Create a salad like a bouquet. Dress it with walnut or hazelnut oil and lemon juice or raspberry vinegar. Either dice the Dolcelatte into the salad or cut it into slices.

Glazed White and Red Currant Tart

6 oz (170g) sweet pastry for base
½ lb (225g) redcurrants, trimmed
½ lb (225g) white currants, trimmed
3 fl oz (85g) dry sherry
3 fl oz (85g) water
4 tablespoons (60ml) quince jelly (redcurrant jelly will do, but is not so good in flavour)

Roll out the pastry to fit a tin size 11 inches (28cm) diameter and 1 inch (2.4cm) deep and bake the case blind. When cool, lay the red and white currants into the tart in alternate stripes.

Mix the sherry with the water and heat, adding the quince jelly until the syrup is smooth. Gently pour over the fruit and leave to set.

Serve with whipped cream or smetana.

*Cool Tomato and Garlic Soup (page 72) and Roulade
of Fresh Garden Pea with Mangetout (page 73).*

August

'When you are in love you are not wise; or,
when you are wise you are not in love.'

Publilius Syrus, *Moral Sayings*
(First Century BC), 816
(tr. Darius Lyman)

The height of summer and we should still be able to eat outdoors, though in Britain, sadly, this is always uncertain. Perhaps, then, a meal in a conservatory so that we are surrounded by plants and green foliage but still dry and warm. For the flower to decorate the table, I have chosen a lily, *L. auratum*, because it is most fragrant and as handsome as any lily could be with its spray of ivory flowers striped in gold, flecked with purple. Design the table in gold and ivory white to reflect the lilies. And what better sound than a classical guitar playing a Bach Suite.

The meal again begins with a cool soup, not too chilled but scented with garlic and garnished with a little chopped basil. Do not be too amazed at the amount of tomatoes needed for this soup for two people — it is pure with no other liquid added.

The main course has a roulade of fresh garden peas with mangetout as the vegetable. Two types of pea, in fact, but their flavour is so different; when the garden pea is made into a purée it becomes the most vivid and appealing shade of green. Since ancient times, the pea has been considered a food for venery purposes, and it crops up in all manner of folk tales. What was the Princess doing, one wonders, if so acutely conscious beneath twenty mattresses of that pea in her bed?

The salad is unusual, but it is a most delicious way of serving baby courgettes. They are eaten raw and moulded into tiny mounds. The Cantal cheese is the oldest French cheese, probably 2000 years old, made from the milk of Salers or Aubrac cows in the Auvergne. It is thought of as the French Cheddar. Fourme de Cantal is eaten in France on special occasions.

Lastly, the dessert of apricots in a vanilla syrup uses another fruit and flavouring long associated with ardour and love-making.

The iced, dry sherry with the soup should refresh the palate for the Bordeaux. And why not linger over the dessert by opening a vintage Sauternes which will be a shade of honey in the candlelight?

Menu

Cool Tomato and Garlic
   Soup

Iced Dry Sherry

Roulade of Fresh Garden
   Pea
Mangetout

St-Estèphe

Courgette Moulds with Red
   Lettuce
Fourme de Cantal

Apricots in Vanilla Syrup

Sauternes

Cool Tomato and Garlic Soup

2 lb (900g) fresh tomatoes
1 head garlic
Sea salt and black pepper
2 tablespoons (30ml) chopped basil

Cook the tomatoes with their skins and the green calyx left on, for this helps the flavour enormously. Either puncture the skin or slice the tomatoes in half. Put them into a saucepan. Peel all the garlic and add to the saucepan. Season. Place over a very low flame and forget about them for 10-15 minutes while they cook in their own juices.

Leave to cool and then push through a sieve, discarding the skin and seeds. Pour the liquid into a bowl and chill in the refrigerator. Bring out half an hour before serving and sprinkle with the chopped basil.

Roulade of Fresh Garden Pea

1 lb (455g) fresh garden peas
¼ pint (140ml) single cream
1 egg, beaten
¼ pint (140ml) curd cheese
Seasoning
Generous handful of mint, finely chopped
¾ lb (340g) puff pastry
Beaten egg for glazing
Sesame seeds

Pod the peas and cook them in a little water until tender. Drain well, then blend with the cream, egg, curd cheese, seasoning and mint.

Roll out the pastry to a square of roughly 12 inches (30cm). Spread the pea mixture over to within ½ inch (12mm) of the edges. Begin to roll the pastry slowly and carefully without pressing down too hard. When you have a roll, place it on a baking sheet, with the edge underneath. Brush with a little beaten egg and sprinkle with sesame seeds.

Bake in a pre-heated oven at 425°F/220°C (Gas Mark 7) for 20-25 minutes, or until the roulade is golden brown and risen. Allow to rest for 10-15 minutes before serving.

Mangetout

Trim ½ lb (225g) of baby mangetout. Steam for 3 minutes. Sprinkle with a little pepper and add a knob of butter.

Courgette Moulds with Red Lettuce

3-4 baby courgettes
Salt
A few leaves of red lettuce
Sesame oil

Trim and then grate the courgettes into a colander. Sprinkle with a little salt. Leave to drain for 30-45 minutes. Place half of them in a small strainer or sieve and press down hard so that all the water is squeezed out and they take the shape of the mould. Invert over a salad plate carefully so that the mould is undisturbed. Repeat with the other half of the grated courgettes.

Decorate this green centre with red leaves of lettuce around it, so that it appears like a flower. Sprinkle the leaves with a little sesame oil.

Serve with slices of the Fourme de Cantal.

Apricots in Vanilla Syrup

2 oz (55g) castor sugar
¼ pint (140ml) water
1 vanilla pod
6 apricots

Add the sugar to the water and stir until it is dissolved. Add the vanilla pod and bring to the boil. Simmer for a few minutes. Add the apricots, sliced in half and with their stones removed. Crack some of the kernels and add to the pan.

Pumpkin and Ginger Soup with Croûtons (page 80).

September

'Can one ever remember love? It's like trying to summon up the smell of roses in a cellar. You might see a rose, but never the perfume.'

Arthur Miller, *After the Fall* (1964)

The evenings are now drawing in and it is dark by the time you dine. There may be a little autumnal chill in the air, so give the dining table a warm look with autumn colours — russet, apple red and gold. Decorate the table with the second growth of roses which now appear in shades of red, orange and yellow.

Saint-Saëns is a highly romantic composer; the violin one of the most moving of all musical instruments. His violin concerto is an inspired piece of music. Play this or one of the Saint-Saëns piano concertos.

The first course stunningly reflects this range of colours, for pumpkin soup is the shade of old gold and this soup in particular is flecked with the darker gold of the ginger. The *croûtons* help the texture as well as adding to the flavour.

Mushrooms are delicious in the autumn and if you can pick your own field mushrooms, so much the better. Devilled mushrooms put a kick into this dish and the mustard sauce is further spiced by the heat of red chillies. Tofu is, of course, rich in protein, which is always stimulating for arduous romantic evenings. Wild rice is not a rice at all but a grass — the flavour is unique.

Chabichou are small goat's cheeses in the shape of truncated cones. They are white and velvety with a firm creamy flavour, particularly good with the strong, slightly bitter crispness of the batavia leaf.

To finish, there is the dark purple richness of the damson ice cream. The colours and flavours have been designed to harmonize and increase a sensual mood.

To drink with the soup, have a Tokay d'Alsace which is made from the black grape used for champagne, which makes a very pale pink wine referred to in France as *vin gris*.

With the main course, treat yourself to one of the great reds, a Margaux, which is smooth and elegant. There are enough vintage years in the Haut-Médoc to choose an excellent Château wine. Finish the meal with a Vouvray to go with the damson ice cream. This can be too intensely sweet for some palates but, at its best, is like golden honey.

Menu

Pumpkin and Ginger Soup   Tokay d'Alsace
  with Croûtons

Stir-fried Smoked Tofu and   Margaux
  Vegetables
Devilled Mushrooms
Wild Rice

Chabichou, Walnut and
  Batavia Salad

Damson Ice Cream   Vouvray

Pumpkin and Ginger Soup
with Croûtons

½ lb (225g) pumpkin flesh
1 oz (30g) ginger root
2 oz (55g) butter
Seasoning
1 pint (570ml) cold water

For the croûtons:

2 slices two-day-old wholemeal bread
1 oz (30g) butter
2 tablespoons (30ml) olive oil
2 cloves garlic, crushed

Chop the pumpkin flesh into cubes and cut away the skin. Peel and grate the ginger root.

Melt the butter in a saucepan and throw in the pumpkin flesh, grated ginger and seasoning. Place over a low heat and simmer gently for 5 minutes. Cover with the cold water. Bring back to the boil and simmer for 10 minutes. Leave to cool and blend to a smooth cream. Reheat gently.

To make the *croûtons*, slice the crusts away from the bread and cut the bread into cubes. Melt the butter with the oil in a frying pan. Throw in the cubed bread and garlic. Sauté briskly for a few minutes until crisp and golden brown. Drain on absorbent paper and serve in a separate bowl.

Stir-fried Smoked Tofu and Vegetables

2 or 3 baby courgettes
2 or 3 baby carrots
7-8 spring onions
4 oz (115g) smoked tofu
2 tablespoons (30ml) corn oil
2 tablespoons (30ml) shoyu sauce
2 tablespoons (30ml) dry sherry or rice wine

Trim and slice the courgettes, carrots and spring onions into lengths roughly 3 inches (8cm) long and slice these into thin strips. Cut and slice the smoked tofu into similarly shaped and sized pieces.

Heat the oil in a wok and throw in the carrots and courgettes. Stir fry for three minutes, then add the tofu. Stir fry for another minute. Add the spring onions, shoyu and sherry or rice wine. Stir fry for another minute. Serve on a platter.

Devilled Mushrooms

1 oz (30g) butter
4 oz (115g) mushrooms, sliced
1 tablespoon (15ml) red wine vinegar
1 dried red chilli, broken
1 tablespoon (15ml) Dijon mustard
1 tablespoon (15ml) Moutarde de Meaux
Sea salt

Melt the butter in a pan. Throw in the mushrooms, vinegar and the red chilli. Sauté gently for a few minutes. When the mushrooms are just cooked, add the two mustards and salt. Stir briskly and serve.

Wild Rice

2 oz (55g) butter
3 oz (85g) wild rice
Sea salt and black pepper

Melt the butter in a pan and add the rice and seasoning. Cover with an inch of water, bring to the boil, then take away from the heat and leave for half an hour. Return to the heat and simmer for 20 minutes, by which time the rice should have absorbed all the liquid. Serve at once.

Chabichou, Walnut and Batavia Salad

1 heart of a Batavia
2 Chabichou cheeses
2 tablespoons (30ml) broken fresh walnuts
1 tablespoon (15ml) lemon juice
4 tablespoons (60ml) walnut oil
Seasoning

Separate the leaves of the batavia and place in a bowl. Place one Chabichou cheese in the centre, whole, and slice the other into rounds and encircle the whole cheese. Sprinkle with the walnuts. Make the vinaigrette with the lemon juice, oil and seasoning. Dress the salad just before serving.

Damson Ice Cream

½ lb (225g) damsons
¼ pint (140ml) brandy
2 eggs, separated
½ pint (285ml) double cream
4 oz (115g) castor sugar

Cook the damsons with the brandy until soft. Leave to cool, then stone them. Purée in a blender. Stir in the egg yolks, then whip the cream until stiff and fold it into the purée.

Whip the egg whites with the sugar and fold this into the fruit purée. Place in an ice-cream maker or deep freeze, but if using the latter, bring the cream out three or four times during the freezing and stir it vigorously to break up the ice crystals.

Burgundy Pears (page 91).

October

'Love is not the dying moan of a distant violin
— it's the triumphant twang of a bedspring.'

S.J. Perelman
(Quoted in A. Andrews, *Quotations for Speakers
and Writers*)

The trees are beginning to turn this month and most of the autumn flowers are rather dire. We do not associate dahlias and chrysanthemums with romance, the latter only with Muriel Spark's memorable phrase from *The Prime of Miss Jean Brodie* — 'such serviceable flowers'. But there are anemones and a small bowl of these on the table, with their brilliant and lustrous colours, can look charming.

Because the autumn colours are so vibrant, I would feel like having the dining table all white. The flowers and the food have enough colour as it is.

The music could be the elegant lyricism of Chopin — his Preludes or Nocturnes.

This meal for two uses tomatoes and mushrooms — seasonal foods associated, too, with love and its arousal. The tomato, in French, is called the 'love apple' and the mushroom has had strong hallucinogenic traditions allied with states of ecstasy.

The first tomatoes to be brought to Europe by the Spaniards were somewhat like the Marmande ones we treasure now and which this recipe uses. But the early ones were even larger, the size of a goose egg, although uneven in shape. There was a yellow variety, given the name of 'golden apple'. The plant was cultivated in gardens for its supposed amorous properties, but rarely eaten as it was considered to smell bad and was also part of the family of the deadly nightshade (which also includes the potato). The tomato was not eaten in any quantity until the eighteenth century, when it was puréed and made into a sauce or soup. The later tomatoes were made into a pickle or jam. In France, they were eaten earlier, cooked whole, and there are many recipes for stuffing them.

Filo pastry can now be bought in supermarkets and delicatessens. Buy it frozen, take out what you need and refreeze the rest; it is both simple and easy to use. Also these individual pies look highly attractive, with their crisp, petalled top and smooth, rounded bottom.

The Pont-l'Evêque cheese has a rich, tangy flavour and should be moist and springy. It is best appreciated when eaten with a simple salad such as that given.

An excellent colour fusion might be to have a pink champagne with the stuffed tomatoes. Sainsbury's now stock a superb one at a reasonable price.

A great wine from the Médoc is St Julien which is dry and flowery, to accompany the main course. Finish the meal with a sharp, dry Calvados to wash down the pears.

Menu

Stuffed Tomatoes   Pink Champagne

Individual Filo Pies   Haut-Médoc
Runner Beans in Pesto
  Sauce
Pink Fir Apple Potatoes

Pont-l'Evêque and Cos
  Lettuce Salad

Burgundy Pears   Calvados

Stuffed Tomatoes

2 large Marmande tomatoes
2 cloves garlic, crushed
1½ tablespoons (22ml) breadcrumbs, toasted
2 tablespoons (30ml) Parmesan cheese, grated
Seasoning
Mint leaves for garnish

Cut the tomatoes in half. Scoop out most of the inside and chop the flesh into a bowl. Squeeze the garlic into the tomato flesh and add the rest of the ingredients.

Pile it all back into the shells and place under a very hot grill. Cook until the inside is bubbling and the cheese quite melted.

Serve after a few minutes, garnished with a mint leaf.

Individual Filo Pies

6 sheets filo pastry
Corn oil
1 oz (30g) butter
1 teaspoon (5ml) crushed coriander
4 oz (115g) mushrooms, sliced
3 oz (85g) curd cheese or Ricotta
6 spring onions, finely chopped
2 tablespoons (30ml) double cream
Seasoning
Beaten egg
Sesame seeds

Use a Yorkshire pudding tin (the sort which has 4-inch (10cm) diameter hollow shapes) and make two pies. Cut the filo sheets in half and then in half again. This gives you 12 small sheets for each pie. Butter two spaces of the tin and arrange two pieces of filo, in a cross, in each space, oiling each sheet and leaving a third overhanging. Then place two more sheets diagonally. Continue with this shape, but brush each sheet with oil before placing the next sheet over.

Meanwhile, melt the butter in a pan and throw in the coriander and mushrooms. Cook over a low flame for a few minutes until the mushrooms are tender. Pour into a bowl and add the curd cheese or Ricotta, onions, double cream and seasoning. Mix well, fill the two pies, then fold over the pastry leaves so that the pies are covered in the filo.

Brush with beaten egg and sprinkle with sesame seeds. Bake in a pre-heated oven at 425°F/220°C (Gas Mark 7) for 20-25 minutes.

Runner Beans in Pesto Sauce

1 lb (455g) runner beans, trimmed
Generous handful of basil leaves
5 tablespoons (75ml) olive oil
Juice of 1 lemon
2 cloves garlic, crushed
2 tablespoons (30ml) pine nuts
1 tablespoon (15ml) Parmesan cheese
Seasoning

Slice the beans into chunks (it is absurd to slice them very thinly) and boil or steam them until tender.

Meanwhile, make the pesto by placing all the basil leaves in a blender with the oil, lemon juice and garlic. Blend until the leaves have become a green sauce. Thicken the sauce by adding the pine nuts and Parmesan cheese. Season carefully.

Turn out the hot beans onto a serving dish and pour the pesto sauce over them.

Pink Fir Apple Potatoes

If you can get these potatoes, then all they need is light boiling. They are the best potato I know, and their season is in the autumn. Small, knobbly and flushed with pink, they look charming as well as tasting superb.

Pont-l'Evêque and Cos Lettuce Salad

Use the heart of a cos lettuce, and cube the cheese. Mix the cut lettuce leaves with walnut oil and lemon juice, then add the cheese to the salad bowl.

Burgundy Pears

2 large pears
¼ pint (140ml) water
2 oz (55g) castor sugar
Rind of 1 lemon
Small piece of cinnamon stick
¼ pint (140ml) burgundy wine
1 teaspoon (5ml) cornflour
2 teaspoons (10ml) cold water

Peel the pears but leave the stalks on. Place the water, sugar, lemon rind and cinnamon stick in a saucepan. Bring to the boil and simmer until the sugar is dissolved. Add the burgundy and bring to the boil again. Place the pears in the syrup so that they are covered. Simmer for 20 minutes, turning the pears once or twice so that they colour evenly. When tender, remove the pears to a glass bowl, reserving the syrup. Discard the lemon rind and cinnamon stick.

Mix the cornflour with the cold water and add to the syrup, heating until it thickens slightly. Pour over the pears and refrigerate for half a day or a full day.

Serve with whipped cream or smetana.

Apple and Cabbage Salad with Brie (page 100) and
Satsumas with Dates (page 101).

November

'When one loves somebody, everything is clear
— where to go, what to do — it all takes care of
itself and one doesn't have to ask anybody
about anything.'

Maxim Gorky, *The Zykovs* (1914), 4

Now that the beginning of winter has arrived and there is more than a nip in the air, one needs warming spiced food to stimulate the circulation.

Make a table decoration of autumn leaves and rose hips — the small scarlet hips look beautiful amongst copper leaves. Dress the table in tawny shades of beige and gold. Play Vivaldi which embraces all the seasons but has a charm and lightness which is a tonic in itself.

Quinces are a wonderful autumnal fruit with a distinct aroma, sharper than lemon and pear mixed together could ever be. Walnuts are fresh now and how different they taste if you eat them soon after they are picked from the tree. Together they make a delicious salad spiced with a little ginger and coriander. The brioche loaf is rich with eggs and butter, but flavoured with celery it is a perfect foil with the spicy salad.

Stuffed pancakes belong to that group of food arranged like a parcel — food which hides its secrets and therefore has its own eroticism.

English apples are so good at this time that I have used them in the salad instead of the dessert, and here they are grated with cabbage and onion. A salad such as this is strong enough to confront and combine with a very ripe Brie.

Satsumas are the first citrus fruit to come in and they are excellent with fresh dates. These are cooked in a syrup which has the addition of rose water.

To go with the spiced quince salad, chill a Beaujolais Nouveau. It is young enough not to quarrel with the spices in the salad and should refresh the palate.

One of the most distinctive white wines in the world is Gewurztraminer from the Alsace. It has a strong, spicy perfume. Make sure you choose a dry one as it can range towards the sweet.

With the pudding, drink a Coteaux de Layon, which is one of the sweet Chenin Blanc wines from Anjou.

Menu

Spiced Quince and Walnut Salad

Beaujolais Nouveau

Stuffed Pancakes with Sweetcorn
Celery Hearts with Herb Butter
Potato Soufflé

Gewürztraminer

Apple and Cabbage Salad with Brie

Satsumas with Dates

Coteaux du Layon

Spiced Quince with Walnut Salad

2 large quinces
1 oz (30g) butter
1 oz (30g) ginger root, peeled and sliced very thinly
1 teaspoon (5ml) coriander, crushed
2 tablespoons (30ml) red wine vinegar
Seasoning
A few leaves of batavia or curly endive
1½ oz (45g) fresh walnuts, shelled and broken up
2 tablespoons (30ml) sour cream

Peel the quinces, cut them in half and core them. Melt the butter in a pan and add the ginger root and coriander. Cook for a moment, then add the quinces, turning them over so that they brown slightly on both sides. Add the wine vinegar and seasoning and simmer with the lid on for 10-12 minutes. Leave to cool in the juice.

To serve, take two plates and lay a few leaves of batavia or curly endive on them. Drain the four halves of quince and place them on top of the salad. Fill the holes in the centre with the walnuts. Mix the sour cream with the spiced juice and pour over the walnuts and quince.

Celery and Cheese Brioche

10 oz (285g) strong white bread flour
4 oz (115g) butter, diced
4 oz (115g) mature Cheddar cheese, grated
1 tablespoon celery salt
1 tablespoon celery seeds
3 eggs, beaten
2 tablespoons milk
1 sachet micronized/active dry yeast

Mix the flour, butter, cheese, celery salt and seeds together. Add the eggs, milk and yeast, mix thoroughly and knead for 5 minutes. If you have dough hooks and a food processor it makes the job easier and quicker. Leave it to rise in a warm place for an hour. Place in a non-stick brioche tin and leave for about 10 minutes, so that the dough rises to the top. Bake in a preheated oven at 190°C/375°F/Gas Mark 5 for 20-25 minutes, until golden brown and crisp on the top. Turn out onto a wire rack and let the brioche cool.

Stuffed Pancakes with Sweetcorn

For the pancakes (makes 4):

2 oz (55g) plain flour
2 oz (55g) buckwheat flour
Pinch of salt
1 egg, lightly beaten
¼ pint (140ml) milk
¼ pint (140ml) water
Sunflower oil for frying

For the filling:

2 corn cobs
2 oz (55g) butter
4 oz (115g) mushrooms, sliced
5 cloves garlic, peeled and sliced
½ teaspoon (2.5ml) mustard seeds
½ teaspoon (2.5ml) asafoetida
½ teaspoon (2.5ml) juniper berries
1 oz (30g) flour
¼ pint (140ml) dry white wine
¼ pint (140ml) single cream

First make the pancakes. Sift the two flours into a bowl. Add the salt and mix in the egg. Slowly add the milk and water until you have a smooth batter. Use a blender for easy results; otherwise, beat the mixture hard. Allow the batter to rest for an hour, then beat again before using.

Heat 1 teaspoon of oil in the pan. Dip a ladle into the batter and gently pour into the pan. Angle the pan so that the pancake mixture runs into a circle. When the top begins to dry out, flip it over and do the other side for a moment. Tip out onto greaseproof paper and reserve. Repeat to make 4 pancakes.

To make the filling, cook the corn cobs in boiling water for 8 minutes or until tender. Allow them to cool, then cut off the kernels and reserve. Melt the butter in a pan, add the mushrooms, garlic and spices, cover and cook for a few moments or until the mushrooms are tender. Work in the flour to make a paste. Cook for a moment, then add the white wine and stir to make a sauce. Add the sweetcorn kernels and fill the pancakes with the stuffing, folding both sides over to form an envelope shape. Carefully lift the pancakes into a shallow oven dish. Dribble over the cream and cook in a pre-heated oven at 400°F/200°C (Gas Mark 6) for 15 minutes.

Celery Hearts with Herb Butter

1 head celery
¼ pint (140ml) vegetable stock
Seasoning
1 tablespoon (15ml) each finely chopped parsley, mint, basil and chives
2 oz (55g) butter, softened

Take off all the outside fibrous stems of celery. Trim the heart at the base and across the stalks at the top. Slice the heart down the centre. Heat the stock in an ovenproof dish. Place the celery in the dish, season, cover with a lid and cook in a pre-heated oven at 400°F/200°C (Gas Mark 6) for 45 minutes. Drain the celery.

Mix the herbs with the butter and spread it over the centre of the celery before serving.

Potato Soufflé

4 oz (115g) potatoes
1 oz (30g) butter
¼ pint (140ml) milk
2 eggs, beaten
Seasoning
2 oz (55g) Gruyère cheese, grated

Boil the potatoes until tender. Mash them, adding the butter, milk, eggs and seasoning. When the mixture is smooth, add the Gruyére cheese. Pour into a small, buttered soufflé dish. Place in a water bath and then cook in a pre-heated oven at 400°F/200°C (Gas Mark 6) for 20 minutes. The top should have risen and be brown.

Apple and Cabbage Salad with Brie

4 oz (115g) white cabbage
2 dessert apples
1 small onion
4 oz (115g) ripe Brie cheese, chopped
2 tablespoons (30ml) extra virgin olive oil
1 teaspoon (5ml) balsamic vinegar
Sea salt and freshly ground black pepper

Grate the cabbage, apples and onion into a bowl. Add the rest of the ingredients, toss well and serve.

Satsumas with Dates

2 oz (55g) castor sugar
¼ pint (140ml) water
2 tablespoons (30ml) rose water
4 satsumas, whole but peeled
5 or 6 dates
Rose petals for garnish

Heat the sugar with the water until the sugar is dissolved. Boil for a few minutes, then add the rose water and the whole satsumas. Simmer for 5 minutes. Chop the dates up very small and throw them into the pan. Leave to cool, then pour into a glass dish and refrigerate for a day.

Decorate the satsumas with small rose petals.

Hot Red Cabbage and Apricot Salad (page 106).

December

'Love is all we have, the only way that each can
help the other.'

Euripedes, *Orestes* (408 BC)
(tr. William Arrowsmith)

If you have spent a lifetime of Christmases with family and friends, it can be a great pleasure to spend a romantic one *à deux*. In decorating the room, I hope there will be a liberal use of mistletoe and that any flower arrangements will be enlivened by scarlet berries and pots of cyclamen in red and white. Carry the colour scheme through to white tablecloth and red napkins and use those Christmas colours of red and white whenever possible.

I suggest also, to help the mood of mad festivity, that you might go in for some show-biz music. I am devoted to Stephen Sondheim's work and the musical *Follies* is full of great numbers which are parodies of the music from various shows. They work on all levels, from tragedy to humour, and a tape of *Side by Side with Sondheim* has many *Follies* numbers (like 'Broadway Baby', 'I'm Still Here', 'I Can't Get You Out of My Mind'), as well as other songs from his musicals. I recommend them because, from personal experience, they work brilliantly in the romantic context. This meal, its wine and its music should topple any fairy from the top of the Christmas tree.

The traditional Christmas feast is heavy, tends to unremitting stodge and is, we now know, very unhealthy. So, break away from tradition entirely and enjoy a meal which is light, spicy and which celebrates the seasonal foods without being high in fat and stodge.

Red cabbage and apricots go very well together, and with the addition of ginger you have a hot, spicy salad which is perfect for stimulating the taste buds at the beginning of the meal.

We need hot, spicy food to warm us in the winter, which is why I have followed the first course with an Indonesian dish, thickened at the last moment with creamed coconut. This curry is fairly mild, though you can regulate its heat according to how many dried chillies you use. It should also be a pale gold in colour, given this shade by the mustard and fenugreek and I have continued this colour scheme by using saffron in the rice.

Citrus fruit is at its initial peak at Christmas, so is chicory, and the first watercress is now available. Mixed together, they make a deliciously refreshing salad. The blue cheese, Bleu de Gex, is unusual and goes brilliantly with the pepper tang of watercress. A cheese from the Franche Comte which is naturally blued, it is creamy white, marbled with deep blue and has a full, rich flavour with a slight edge to it.

The individual tartlets to end the meal look so enticing, as good as anything in Paris *Pâtisserie* windows and not in the least difficult to make. Serve them with a little whipped cream, smetana or Greek yogurt.

To drink with this meal, why not start with a beautiful dry and light Italian wine that sparkles in the glass like Champagne. Then continue with one of my favourite wines, that slightly smoky but fragrant Pouilly-Fumé made from the Sauvignon white grape. One has to take care with the wine when eating spicy dishes, but this curry is mild and slightly creamy, so if the Pouilly-Fumé is chilled rather more than usual, its fragrance will stand up beautifully and slightly undercut the spices in the dish.

As it is Christmas, why not open one of the great dessert wines, the only white wine to be given the rank of *grand premier cru*–the finest Sauternes, Château d'Yquem. But if that is too wildly expensive, choose another Sauternes from a good vintage ('75, '76, '79, '81).

Menu

Hot Red Cabbage and
  Apricot Salad

Malvasia Secco di
  Carmiano

Indonesian Vegetable Curry
Saffron Rice

Pouilly-Fumé

Chicory, Watercress and
  Orange Salad
Bleu de Gex

Grape Tartlets

Château d'Yquem (or
  another Sauternes)

Hot Red Cabbage and Apricot Salad

2 tablespoons (30ml) corn oil
1 oz (30g) ginger root, grated
3 cloves garlic
¼ red cabbage, sliced thinly
1 tablespoon (15ml) brown sugar
¼ pint (140ml) red wine vinegar
Seasoning
1 tablespoon (15ml) raisins
1 tablespoon (15ml) currants
2 tablespoons (30ml) brandy
2 oz (55g) dried apricots, soaked overnight
2 tablespoons (30ml) Brazil nuts, broken

Heat the oil in a casserole and sweat the ginger root and garlic. Throw in the red cabbage and add the sugar, vinegar and seasoning. Place a lid on the casserole and cook in a warm oven at 350°F/180°C (Gas Mark 4) for 2 hours.

Meanwhile, soak the raisins and currants in the brandy and simmer the soaked apricots in their soaking water for 15 minutes. Drain. Then chop the apricots, add them to the cabbage with the marinated raisins and currants and their juice. Give a good stir and allow to cool. Make the day before and allow to stand for 24 hours.

Reheat it, stirring briskly and adding freshly-milled pepper. Serve the salad on individual plates and scatter with a little of the chopped nuts.

Indonesian Vegetable Curry

3 tablespoons (45ml) corn oil
1 teaspoon (5ml) mustard seeds
1 teaspoon (5ml) fenugreek pieces
½ teaspoon (2.5ml) each cumin, cardamom and asafoetida
Small piece of tamarind and cassia
2 dried red chillies, chopped
2 small carrots, peeled and chopped
2 small parsnips, peeled and chopped
2 small onions, peeled and chopped
2 small turnips, peeled and chopped
4 oz (115g) mushrooms, thinly sliced
4 oz (115g) potatoes, peeled and chopped
Sea salt
2 oz (55g) creamed coconut, grated
Handful of coriander leaves, chopped

Heat the oil in a pan and throw in the spices. Sauté them for a moment or until the mustard seeds begin to pop. Throw in all the vegetables, season, give a good stir, let them cook for a moment before adding enough water to cover. Bring to the boil and simmer for 20 minutes. Take away from the heat and stir in the grated coconut.

Sprinkle with the coriander leaves and pour into a tureen to serve.

Saffron Rice

1 oz (30g) butter
1 teaspoon (5ml) saffron threads
3 oz (85g) Patna rice
Seasoning

In a pan, melt the butter and add the saffron and then the rice. Sauté the rice, stirring it, for a few minutes. Barely cover with water, season, then place a lid on the pan and simmer over a low flame for 10 minutes. After this time, all the water should have been absorbed.

Turn out the rice into a colander and briefly dry it in a low oven before serving.

Chicory, Watercress and Orange Salad

1 orange
1 head chicory
½ bunch watercress
1 teaspoon (5ml) lemon juice
Seasoning
2 tablespoons (30ml) walnut oil

Peel the orange. Remove all the pith and slice the orange across in circles. (Drink the juice.) Divide the chicory into separate leaves, slicing the bigger ones down the centre. Cut the watercress sprigs from their stalks and toss with the chicory and orange.

Mix the lemon juice, seasoning and walnut oil together and toss the salad in the dressing just before serving.

The Bleu de Gex goes particularly well with citrus fruit and a slightly peppery leaf like watercress. Cut into slices to serve.

Grape Tartlets

Try to get seedless black and white grapes for this recipe. The small Muscat grapes (Thompson's Seedless) are in the shops before Christmas. If not, you will have to take out the seeds from the grapes before making the tarts.

For the pastry:

2½ oz (70g) butter
4 oz (115g) flour
½ tablespoon (8ml) icing sugar
Pinch of salt
1 egg yolk
2 tablespoons (30ml) iced water

For the filling:

4 tablespoons (60ml) fromage frais
4 oz (115g) white grapes
4 oz (115g) black grapes
4 tablespoons (60ml) apple jelly
3 fl oz (90ml) dry sherry
1 tablespoon (15ml) castor sugar

Refrigerate the butter so that it is ice cold. Sift the flour, add the icing sugar and salt. Grate the butter into it and rub the flour and fat together until the mixture resembles fine breadcrumbs. Mix the egg yolk with the water and stir it into the mixture until you have a smooth paste. Wrap in greaseproof paper and refrigerate for an hour.

Roll out the dough and cut four circles to fit a tart tin. Bake blind until golden brown. Take out and cool.

Fill each tart with *fromage frais*, then cover two of the tarts with white grapes in a circular pattern and the remaining two with the black grapes.

Melt the apple jelly with the dry sherry until you have a smooth syrup. Pour gently over the four tarts so that the grapes are covered. Sprinkle with a little castor sugar.

*Roulade of Spinach and Blue Cheese (page 120) with
various salads and Passion-fruit Jelly (page 121).*

the Engagement *party*

Fill the room with yellow and white roses, play the most romantic music in the background. I suggest Jessye Norman singing Richard Strauss's Four Last Songs, but play romantic music for all tastes from Piaf to Blues.

As there are four dishes plus salads for the main course, I suggest an hors-d'oeuvre which is simple — a pile of quail eggs built up in a cone shape with sesame salt to dip into and a platter of *crudités* with a herb purée. And would it much matter if some of the *crudités* were a little phallic shaped, or that their preparation made them more so?

Drink champagne to begin with — what else? But follow with a light Californian Chardonnay and perhaps, if the price is not too steep, go for a gentle, mellow burgundy, a *premier cru*, a Nuits-St-Georges — this has a velvety warmth with a touch of spice, just the wine to add zest to an engagement party. Choose from Domaine de la Romanée-Conti or the vineyards of Vosne-Romanée which are somewhat cheaper to buy. Hungarian Tokay goes well with the dessert.

A Buffet for Thirty

Quail Eggs with Sesame
  Salt
Crudités and Fresh Herb
  Purée

Champagne

West Indian Casserole
Omelette Gâteau
Timbales de Crêpes
Roulade of Spinach and
  Blue Cheese

Californian Chardonnay

Nuits-St-Georges

Salads

Passion-fruit Jelly
Green Chartreuse Ice
  Cream

Hungarian Tokay

Quail Eggs

Gently place batches of 10 quail eggs (you will need about 100 altogether) in a saucepan. Fill with cold water, bring to the boil, then turn the heat off, cover the pan and let them stay in the water until cold. Do not peel the eggs as their charm rests so much in their speckled shells. Arrange on a traditional ham stand in a cone shape.

Sesame Salt

Use ½ lb (225g) of sesame seeds and roast them in a dry saucepan. You will need to divide this amount into three for, if you roast too many at one time, some might burn. Shake the saucepan over a flame until some of the seeds pop and they all turn a dark gold in colour. Place the seeds, when cool, in a blender and whizz until they have become a powder. Add one part sea salt to seven parts of sesame powder. Mix well. Serve in an attractive dish, even a traditional salt cellar.

Crudités

Choose from strips of carrot, peppers, cucumber, raw asparagus, courgettes, tomatoes and cauliflower florets.

Fresh Herb Purée

Use parsley, chives and mint; also, if you have them, celery leaves, lovage and chervil. Mix equal parts of *fromage frais* and smetana together. Add finely chopped fresh herbs and a little salt and black pepper to give the purée a speckled and dark green appearance.

West Indian Casserole

6 oz (170g) chick-peas, soaked overnight
6 oz (170g) dried black beans, soaked overnight
3 tablespoons (45ml) corn oil
2 oz (55g) ginger root, peeled and gratea
5 cloves garlic, crushed
1 teaspoon (5ml) cumin seeds
1 teaspoon (5ml) mustard seeds
1 teaspoon (5ml) cloves
1 teaspoon (5ml) turmeric
2 sticks cinnamon
3 onions, chopped coarsely
2 lb (1 kilo) potatoes, peeled and chopped
1 white cabbage, chopped
1 cauliflower, broken into florets
4 tablespoons (60ml) tomato paste
1 teaspoon (5ml) sea salt
3 oz (85g) creamed coconut, grated

Boil the chick-peas in plenty of fresh water for 2 hours or cook in a pressure cooker for 20 minutes. Separately, boil the black beans fiercely for 10 minutes. Throw away the water and begin cooking again in fresh water. Simmer for 1 hour or until tender. Reserve both the cooked chick-peas and black beans, together with their water.

Heat the corn oil and throw in the ginger, garlic and all the spices. Sweat these for a moment, then add the onions, beans, potatoes and cabbage, together with the water from the pulses. Bring to the boil and simmer for 15 minutes. Add the cauliflower, tomato paste and salt. Simmer for 5 minutes, then add the cooked chick-peas and black beans. Stir and simmer for a further 3 minutes. Stir in the creamed coconut and simmer for 2 more minutes. Leave to cool.

This dish is best made the day before and reheated on the day.

Omelette Gâteau

12 eggs, beaten
Generous bunch of parsley, finely chopped
3 oz (85g) butter
4 oz (115g) Cheddar or Gruyère cheese, grated
Sea salt and freshly ground black pepper
½ lb (225g) leeks, trimmed and sliced
2 tablespoons (30ml) sour cream or fromage frais
2 red peppers, cored, seeded and sliced
4 tomatoes, skinned
1 onion, sliced
3 cloves garlic, crushed
3 tablespoons (45ml) olive oil
1 avocado (not ripe), peeled and sliced
4 oz (115g) mangetout, trimmed
2 oz (55g) Parmesan cheese, grated

Mix the eggs with the parsley, cheese and 1 oz (30g) of the butter. Using another 1 oz (30g) of the butter, make four omelettes and reserve them by covering each one with greaseproof paper.

Cook the leeks in the rest of the butter until they are soft and then place in the blender to make a rough purée, adding the sour cream or *fromage frais*. Cook the peppers, onion and garlic together in the olive oil for about 15 minutes. Add the tomatoes and cook for a further five minutes until you have a rough purée. Steam the mangetout for 3 minutes, adding the avocado for the last minute.

Place one omelette on a well-buttered baking sheet. Cover with the leek purée, then another omelette, followed by the ratatouille mixture covered with another omelette. Finally, cover with the mangetout and avocado mixture and the last omelette. Sprinkle with Parmesan cheese and cook in pre-heated oven at 350°F/180°C (Gas Mark 4) for 15 minutes.

Cut like a cake to serve.

Timbales de Crêpes

These are moulded pancakes cooked in a soufflé dish and interleaved with various purées and custards. Cook the components separately as follows:

Crêpe Batter (makes 10)

4 oz (115g) plain flour
2 eggs
½ pint (285ml) skimmed milk
3 tablespoons (45ml) yogurt
1 teaspoon (5ml) each salt and garam masala
1 tablespoon (15ml) sunflower oil

Sift the flour. Beat the eggs into it and then add the rest of the ingredients, beating well. Allow the batter to rest for an hour.

Oil a pan, heat it, and ladle enough batter into the pan to cover the base with a thin layer. Cook, turn the crêpe, and just let that side dry out before laying the crêpe on a piece of greaseproof paper. Continue until you have used all the batter.

Spinach Sauce

1 lb (455g) spinach
1 oz (30g) butter
Pinch of nutmeg
Sea salt and black pepper
1 oz (30g) plain flour
2 oz (55g) grated Gruyère cheese
2 eggs

Tear the washed spinach leaves into small pieces. Pat them dry in a cloth and place in a saucepan with the butter, nutmeg, salt and pepper. Let the spinach reduce over a low heat for five minutes. Add the flour, stir, then add the cheese. Remove from the heat and when cool, beat in the eggs.

Mushroom Duxelles

1 lb (455g) mushrooms, sliced
2 small chopped onions
1 tablespoon (15ml) olive oil
Salt and freshly ground black pepper
3 tablespoons (45ml) chopped parsley

Cook the mushrooms with the onions in the olive oil. When they start to lose their moisture, raise the heat and stir continuously, so that the liquid is evaporated. Watch that they do not burn. They must be cooked and dry. Add a little salt, pepper and the parsley when they are cooked.

Leek Custard

1 lb (455g) leeks
1 tablespoon (15ml) olive oil
1 egg
2 oz (55g) curd cheese
Salt and freshly ground pepper

Slice the leeks down the centre, clean them and cut across into ½-inch (12mm) slices. Cook them in the oil over a low heat until they are soft. Allow to cool. Blend in a liquidizer with the egg and cheese and a little salt and pepper.

To assemble the timbale:

Butter an 8-inch (20-cm) soufflé dish. Take 4 crêpes and arrange them around the sides, allowing about 1 inch (2.5cm) to sit on the bottom and as much as possible at the top. Place one crêpe at the bottom of the dish and cover with some of the spinach sauce. Place a crêpe over it and add the mushroom *duxelles*, then another crêpe and the leek custard. You may have room for two or three more layers. Do not feel you have to use up all of the sauces. When the soufflé dish is full, fold over the side crêpes so that they meet at the top and cover with another crêpe.

Put a piece of foil over the top, sit the soufflé dish in a roasting tin filled with boiling water and cook in a pre-heated oven at 400°F/200°C (Gas Mark 6) for one hour. Take the *timbale* out of the oven and let it rest for five minutes before unmoulding onto a warm platter.

Serve by cutting like a cake into wedges.

Roulade of Spinach and Blue Cheese

1½ lb (680g) spinach leaves, spines removed
1 onion, finely chopped
1 oz (30g) butter
1 oz (30g) flour
¼ pint (140ml) skimmed milk
½ teaspoon (2.5ml) nutmeg
Black pepper
5 oz (140g) blue cheese (Gorgonzola or Roquefort)
¾ lb (340g) frozen puff pastry, thawed
1 egg, beaten
Sesame seeds for garnish

Wash the spinach thoroughly and cook with the onion in a large saucepan over a gentle heat with no added water until the spinach is one third of its original bulk — about 5 minutes. Squeeze out any excess liquid and break the leaves up with a wooden spoon. Place in a mixing bowl.

Melt the butter in a small saucepan and, when foaming, add the flour. Cook, stirring constantly for 2 minutes. Add the milk, nutmeg and a little black pepper and beat well. Drop in the cheese, bit by bit, and stir into the sauce until it is fairly smooth. Leave to cool, then beat the cheese sauce into the spinach so that you have a thick, chunky, green paste.

Roll out the pastry to form a 12 × 8 inch (30 × 20cm) rectangle. Spread the paste over the pastry, leaving ½-inch (12mm) around the edges. Roll up carefully and place on a buttered baking tray with the join underneath. Seal the ends. Brush with beaten egg and sprinkle with sesame seeds. Bake at 400°F/200°C (Gas Mark 6) for about 40 minutes or until puffed up and golden brown.

Leave to stand for 5 minutes before slicing.

Salads

Make various salads to go with these four main courses: have a green salad which includes rocket and dandelion leaves with the crisp lettuce; a young spinach salad with sorrel and nasturtium leaves and flowers; a mixed red-leaf salad of radiccio and red chicory with Chinese mustard greens and flowers.

Toss these with various dressings which use walnut oil and lime, balsamic vinegar and basil oil and a whole mustard-seed dressing with olive oil and red wine vinegar.

Passion-fruit Jelly

Make these in individual jelly moulds. Scoop out the flesh and juice of about 25 passion-fruit and place in a blender. Whizz for a second or two.

In a saucepan, take a handful of carrageen (Irish moss) and simmer in one pint (570ml) of water for 5 minutes. Carefully sieve the liquid and squeeze out all the moisture from the moss. Add to the liquid three tablespoons (45ml) of castor sugar and heat again until the sugar is dissolved. Pour in the passion-fruit pulp. Mix thoroughly. Pour into the moulds and refrigerate until needed.

Green Chartreuse Ice Cream

(Serves 8, so multiply amounts by 3)

6 egg yolks
½ lb (225g) castor sugar
2 tablespoons (30ml) grated lime zest
3 fl oz (90ml) water
3 tablespoons (45ml) green chartreuse
1 pint (570ml) double cream

Whisk egg yolks until thick. Mix sugar, lime zest and water together. Gently bring to the boil, stirring to dissolve the sugar. Pour the syrup onto the egg yolks and whisk for 10 minutes or so, until you have a smooth, thick sauce. Add the green chartreuse. Whisk the cream until thick, then fold the two mixtures together. Freeze.

*Assorted Moulds (pages 126-127), Green Salad
(page 129) and Exotic Fruit Salad (page 130).*

the Wedding breakfast

I suggest we begin the party by serving Kir Royale, champagne with a little cassis. The music is the choice of the bride, but the most stunning wedding I have been to used colours of white and gold for decoration and the sounds in the background were those of harp music, almost the ultimate lyricism — though whether the bride and bridegroom ever heard it is a moot point.

This is a sit-down meal and the moulds (the amounts in this recipe need to be multiplied by five) can be cut up and arranged in various patterns on individual plates, to be garnished with fresh asparagus that has been poached briefly for 2-3 minutes. Decorate each plate with a small seasonal flower or petal and choose one which is edible, for all garnishes should be eaten.

To drink with this course have a New Zealand Pouilly-Fuissé — these new white wines from New Zealand are amazingly good; they have a strength and body to them without being at all acid or going to the other extreme and becoming too fruity. With the main course, drink a strong red, a heady fruity wine like a Spanish Rioja. To go with the dessert, there is only one wine — a Monbazillac, unless the bride has a millionaire father, in which case you drink Château d'Yquem.

A Formal Party for Fifty

Assorted Moulds

New Zealand
    Pouilly-Fuissé

Oyster Mushroom Filo Pie
Green Peppercorn and
    Potato Croquettes
Mangetout

Spanish Rioja

Green Salad

Exotic Fruit Salad

Monbazillac

Assorted Moulds

2 nori sheets
2 tablespoons (30ml) soy sauce (shoyu)
2 large lettuce leaves
2 large spinach leaves

For the fillings:

Spiced Beetroot

3 raw beetroot, grated
1 teaspoon (5ml) paprika
Pinch of cayenne
2 tablespoons (30ml) Crema di Pomodoro (available from Neals Yard, Covent Garden, London and delicatessens)
1 tablespoon (15ml) curd cheese

Mix everything together to form a rough paste.

Cauliflower and Avocado

½ small caulifower
1 ripe avocado
3 cloves garlic, crushed
Generous handful of parsley, finely chopped
2 or 3 lovage leaves, finely sliced
Sea salt and black pepper
3 fl oz (90ml) sour cream
2 oz (55g) softened butter

Break up the cauliflower into florets and boil or steam until just tender. Allow to cool and chop coarsely. Peel and dice the avocado.

Place all the ingredients in a large mixing bowl and mix thoroughly.

Avocado and Potato

1 ripe avocado
½ lb (225g) potatoes, boiled and diced
Handful of dill, finely sliced
3 fl oz (90ml) sour cream
2 oz (55g) softened butter
Sea salt and freshly ground black pepper

Peel and dice the avocado. Add to the rest of the ingredients and mix thoroughly.

To assemble the moulds:

Moisten the nori sheets in the soy sauce so that they are pliable. Use to line a mould or small ramekin and fill with the spiced beetroot mixture. Close up the nori and refrigerate the mould for 24 hours.

Blanch the lettuce and spinach leaves and line a mould with each variety in the same way as above. Use the cauliflower and avocado mixture with the spinach leaves, and the avocado and potato mixture with the lettuce.

All moulds are refrigerated for a day. They can be served whole, or cut into wedges and a selection arranged on individual plates.

Oyster Mushroom Filo Pie

(Five of these pies will be enough for 50 people.)

½ lb (225g) dried fungi, sliced
¼ pint (140ml) dry white wine
2 oz (55g) butter
1 lb (455g) oyster mushrooms
½ lb (225g) okra, trimmed
1 oz (30g) plain flour
¼ pint (140ml) single cream
Sea salt and freshly ground black pepper
1 lb (455g) filo pastry
2 oz (55g) butter, melted
3 tablespoons (45ml) finely chopped parsley
1 egg, beaten
2 tablespoons (30ml) almonds, roughly crushed

Soak the dried fungi in the white wine overnight. Melt 1 oz (30g) of butter in a pan and add the oyster mushrooms and okra. Sauté gently for 5 minutes. Drain the fungi, carefully saving the liquor, and add the fungi to the pan. Continue cooking gently for another five minutes. Leave to cool and drain the juices into the white wine liquor. Melt another 1 oz (30g) of butter and add the flour to make a roux. Add the white wine liquor and single cream. Stir until you have a smooth sauce. Season to taste.

Butter a large, shallow, ovenproof dish. Lay the first filo sheet into it, brush with melted butter, scatter a little parsley over it and lay another sheet of filo into the dish so that it comes up one side. Butter and scatter parsley over that. Continue with two-thirds of the packet of filo, building up the four sides of the pie and interleaving most of the sheets with melted butter and parsley.

Lay the mushrooms, fungi and okra into the pie, pour over the sauce, cover the top with the rest of the layers of filo, tucking in the ends so that the pie is covered. Interleave these sheets with more melted butter and parsley. When all the pastry is used up, glaze the top with beaten egg and scatter with the chopped almonds. Bake in a pre-heated oven, 375°F/190°C (Gas Mark 5) for 25-30 minutes.

Remove from the oven and allow to settle for 5-8 minutes before slicing.

Green Peppercorn and Potato Croquettes

(These quantities will make 20 croquettes. For 50 people, you need 2 croquettes each, which will take 15 lb (6.8kg) of potatoes.)

3 lb (1.36kg) potatoes, peeled
½ lb (225g) mature Cheddar cheese, grated
Sea salt and freshly ground black pepper
4 tablespoons (60ml) green peppercorns
Plain flour
1 egg, beaten
Brown breadcrumbs, to coat
Sunflower oil, for frying

Boil the potatoes until they are tender. Drain and mash them, adding the grated Cheddar and seasoning — be generous with the black pepper. Then stir in the green peppercorns. Roll into balls and then into sausage shapes about 3 inches (75mm) long. Refrigerate for an hour.

Cover with flour, dip in beaten egg and roll in the breadcrumbs. Refrigerate until needed, then deep-fry in hot sunflower oil until brown and crisp.

Mangetout, steamed for 2 minutes, make a delicious accompaniment to the meal.

Green Salad

A green salad made up with a crisp lettuce like Little Gem, together with rocket and claytonia leaves, would refresh the palate after such richness. The dressing should be simple too, using the best extra virgin olive oil with lemon juice.

Exotic Fruit Salad

Use a mixture of papaya, passion-fruit, rambutan, star apple, guava, mango, mangosteen and pineapple. They need no added sugar, or syrup, for once cut up they make plenty of juice. So merely prepare the salad and refrigerate. I would suggest no cream and serve on individual plates, for the fruit looks very attractive and such a salad is the most refreshing conclusion to a meal.

'Leave the dishes for the morning, darling.'

S

T

V

W